Since Sliced Bread

Since Sliced Bread is a national call for common-sense ideas that will strengthen our economy and improve the lives of working families. It began with a contest seeking the best kitchen-table ideas to grow the economy and help workers and companies prosper. **Since Sliced Bread** seeks to be a forum for ordinary Americans, who are rarely asked for their ideas, to offer their own and to change the way policy ideas emerge.

For more information, go to http://www.sinceslicedbread.com.

Since Sliced Bread

COMMON-SENSE IDEAS FROM AMERICA'S WORKING FAMILIES

Foreword by Andy Stern

Preface by Bill Bradley, Mellody Hobson, and Ed Rollins

Photos by Earl Dotter

Don Stillman, Editor

Chelsea Green Publishing, White River Junction, Vermont

Gina Glantz, Project Director

Don Stillman, Editor
Design by Katerina Barry: http://www.katerinabarry.com/design
Principal photography by Earl Dotter, copyright © 2007: http://www.earldotter.com
Research by Doe Bay Institute: http://www.doebayinstitute.org
Production by Big Oak Media: http://www.bigoakmedia.org

Printed in the United States of America.

First printing, January 2007

Library of Congress Cataloging-in-Publication Data

Since sliced bread : common sense ideas from America's working families /
edited by Don Stillman ; foreword by Andy Stern ; preface by Bill Bradley,
Mellody Hobson, and Ed Rollins ; photos by Earl Dotter.
p.cm.
Includes bibliographical references and index

ISBN: 978-1-933392-60-8
(ISBN-10: 1-933392-60-6)

1. United States--Social policy--1993- 2. United States--Economic
policy--2001- 3. Social Change--United States. I. Stillman, Donald Dennis,
1945- II. Title
HN65.S5624 2007   362.85'5610973--dc22   2007000296

Chelsea Green Publishing
P.O. Box 428
White River Junction, VT 05001
(800) 639-4099
www.chelseagreen.com

Acknowledgments

The **Since Sliced Bread** community owes thanks to many people who have helped create some of the best ideas since, well, since sliced bread. First and foremost, Andy Stern, the president of the Service Employees International Union (SEIU), has been the great inspiration for insisting that America's working families need to be listened to by the powers that be in government, business, and labor. He championed the notion that most people in America's heartland have common-sense ideas about what needs to be done to improve lives in our 21st century global economy. And he would be the first to note the support for **Since Sliced Bread** from Anna Burger, who is SEIU secretary-treasurer and chair of the Change To Win labor federation; Mary Kay Henry, Gerry Hudson, Eliseo Medina, and Tom Woodruff, SEIU executive vice-presidents; and the entire SEIU Executive Board.

A group of 23 distinguished judges donated their time and wisdom to evaluating ideas submitted to the contest. They came from business, government, public interest groups, academia, non-profits and also from the right and the left, from Democratic and Republican administrations, and from truly a wide range of backgrounds, professions, skills, and views. Thanks to: Bill Bradley, Carol M. Browner, Louis E. Caldera, Gail C. Christopher, Brian Dabson, Lloyd H. Dean, Amy L. Domini, Esther Dyson, Jeff Faux, Bill Frenzel, Mellody Hobson, Alan Khazei, Donna Klein, Charles E. M. Kolb, Wendy Kopp, Ginger Lew, Martha Phillips, Carl Pope, Edward J. Rollins, David K. Shipler, David L. Sifry, and Kathryn Wylde.

Thanks go also to Gina Glantz, Senior Advisor to SEIU President Stern, whose creative skills and political savvy shaped **Since Sliced Bread** from the very onset. Cheryl Parker Rose also helped guide the project. Ben Sachs provided legal counsel. Rhonda Pitts provided support that was invaluable, as did Alexis Rodich, executive assistant to Gina Glantz.

The **Since Sliced Bread** website and Internet presence was developed by the team at EchoDitto, including Nicco Mele, Michael Silberman, and Terence Heath. Their brilliant work helped bring about the huge outpouring of participants who submitted their ideas and debated them online.

Along the way, **Since Sliced Bread** benefited from a wide range of bloggers, including Andrei Cherny, Glenn Reynolds, Amy Sullivan, and Marshall Wittman. Thanks also to Lisa Lederer, Gretchen Wright, and Johanna Diaz of PR Solutions as well as Will Robinson, Tierney Hunt, and Lori Lodes at MacWilliams, Robinson, and Partners.

SEIU also thanks those who prepared the great book you're reading. Don Stillman served as editor, while principal photography came from Earl Dotter. Katerina Barry did the graphic design. Eli Staub fact-checked the book. The Doe Bay Institute provided research and Big Oak Media did production work. Jocelyn Augustino photographed a number of the top 21 contestants.

Most of all, thanks go to all those who submitted the 22,000 common-sense ideas—the best of which form the core of **Since Sliced Bread**. And thanks to the thousands of others who critiqued, praised, attacked, or otherwise commented on those ideas and enhanced the debate. The stars of **Since Sliced Bread** are on the pages that follow, particularly the top 21 winners whom you will meet and whose ideas you'll engage. The winning idea can be found on page 19 and the two runners-up follow. Ideas 4-21 all were finalists and follow in random order. The biographical information on the winners reflects their occupations and activities at the time they won in 2006. For more detail on the ideas, we urge you to explore the resources and groups cited in footnotes at the end of the book. The factoids and supplemental materials are drawn from these sources and they deserve full credit for their original research.

Finally, we must note that, while we've done our best to ensure accuracy and fairness throughout, we apologize for any errors that may have crept in and note that such shortcomings are not the responsibility of the judges, SEIU leaders, funders, or contributors. And the great variety of ideas in this book means inevitably that not all the people involved in the project agree with each and every idea.

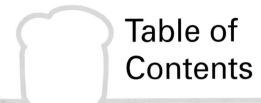

Table of Contents

Foreword

By Andy Stern
President, Service Employees International Union

This book—and the project that gave birth to it—emerged from the frustration my union felt in watching the 2004 presidential campaign go forward. As president of the Service Employees International Union, I spend much of my time talking with American workers about their concerns and their lives.

They are facing the brunt of huge economic changes, but our government has done very little to help them deal with these transformations—and has often made their jobs harder. Incomes for those in the middle class have stagnated despite the fact that Americans are bone-tired from working harder than ever. Jobs are less secure and poverty is on the rise. Much of what we were once told about what the American Dream represents is quickly slipping away.

And yet both parties in Washington spent far too much time arguing over side issues and ignoring the real challenges affecting everyday Americans. It's no surprise that the frustration I felt was shared by many.

Rather than be satisfied with griping and hand-wringing, the union I am fortunate enough to head decided to do something about it. We knew that the old answers on what was needed to help workers were out-of-touch and out-of-date. But we also knew that we would never find the new answers if we simply went back to the same old people.

So instead of relying on the experts found at the top of ivory towers or inside the Beltway, we decided to try something that had never truly been attempted before on a big scale: looking for new ideas from the bottom up, instead of handing them from the top down.

It used to be that decisions about economic policy happened among a small group of people whose well-heeled feet graced the marble halls of Capitol Hill or the plush corridors of the West Wing.

Our idea was that if we want change for the American people, let's ask the American people. . . for a change.

We took our inspiration in part from the flood of new television shows over the past few years that search for unknown talent that might otherwise never be discovered. If "American Idol" could find the next pop singer and "America's Next Top Model" could discover the next star on the fashion runway, why not have a contest to find the next big idea that would improve the lives of American workers?

Thanks to the Internet, today we could do just that. We settled on the name "**Since Sliced Bread**" for our contest because it captured what we were looking for: practical ideas that would make a real difference. We offered a prize of $100,000 for the best idea and two $50,000 prizes for the runners-up. And then we threw open the doors of the contest to see what would happen.

At first our worry was whether we could connect with enough Americans out there who could afford to spend the time to write up a thoughtful idea and submit it. We decided that if we could get 500 people to actually take a few minutes and think hard about what kinds of innovative policies America needed to adopt, we could clearly call it a success—and avoid being embarrassed. Among ourselves, we secretly wondered what would happen if the interest grew and we got up to 5,000 submissions. But we didn't let ourselves spend too much time thinking about whether this could actually happen.

On October 5, 2005, the contest launched. At first there was a trickle of ideas, but it began to grow into a stream and very quickly it became a flood. And then the flood gathered momentum. Some of the ideas were revolutionary, others were ridiculous. But they all sparked debate and discussion and new thinking and more new ideas.

By the time the period to enter ideas into the contest had ended two months later, more than 22,000 ideas had been submitted by Americans—from all over the country and all walks of life—for improving the economy and people's lives. In addition, more than a hundred thousand others joined the discussion and decisions over which ideas worked best and where America needed to go.

Ultimately, ideas went to a blue-ribbon panel of judges. These judges included former U.S. Senator Bill Bradley and Ed Rollins, who managed President Reagan's campaign. There was a former Administrator of the Environmental Protection Agency and a former Secretary of the Army. In fact, there were members of the past four Administrations. But it wasn't just government leaders. We had Internet entrepreneurs and health care CEOs, the founder of Teach for America, the Executive Director of the Sierra Club and the former Executive Director of the Concord Coalition, writers and policy wonks, academics, and activists. They weren't exactly Simon Cowell, but they were a pretty tough group of judges. After a lot of work, they settled on the top 21 entries—21 ideas for the 21st century.

And then the thousands of members of the online **Sliced Bread** community took over. They argued and debated and discussed and were in no way shy about sharing their opinions. And when the Internet voting was done, they had selected the number one idea and two runners-up.

There's more about the top 21 ideas in the pages to follow, but before you get to them, I wanted to share a few broader thoughts about the lessons we learned:

First, Americans are hungry to participate and make their voices heard. Maybe it was the $100,000 grand prize that sucked people in. But in the comments on the active discussion boards that sprung up overnight, it seemed to be much more than that. Not everyone could score a record deal or look good in a bikini, but here was a contest where everybody in America had something to contribute. And it was one where everybody felt they had a stake. People are sick of being ignored by a Washington political process that often seems to be about everything other than Americans' daily lives and struggles. They got their chance to speak up and offer their insights. Maybe their voices couldn't hit a high C, but they got heard in Washington and helped to jumpstart the discussion of a new economic agenda for a new century.

Second, Americans know we need new ideas. Throughout the conversation on **Since Sliced Bread**, there was a strong sense of dissatisfaction with the direction that America was taking and a conviction that we had become disconnected from the values that once made our economy work. Bubbling over with enthusiasm and proposals, the members of the **Sliced Bread** community spent little time complaining about where things were headed compared to the amount of energy they devoted to finding original and creative ways to put America on a better track.

Third, Americans have many concerns that are not on Washington's agenda. One of the most valuable parts of the **Since Sliced Bread** experience was that it offered a window onto the concerns Americans were thinking about that are far off of Washington D.C.'s radar screen. For instance, there was the sense among many of the participants that average Americans should have more information about and more of a say on where their tax dollars are spent. While neither political party in Congress is speaking adequately to those concerns, the contest featured multiple ideas on how citizens can have more control and decision-making power over what government does and how it does it when it comes to our tax code.

Fourth, Americans are focused on what works, not on pat political answers. While pundits may be convinced that Americans are divided red and blue, most of the ideas in **Since Sliced Bread** were far more difficult to stick into the corners of conventional ideology. They were, in a word, purple. There were, of course, the fair share of submissions that can be characterized by the old stereotypes of "big government liberalism" and "tax cutting conservatism."

But many more of the ideas were not so easy to pigeonhole. For instance, among the top 21 ideas, there were proposals to make the Social Security tax flat in a way that makes it more progressive and to give workers ownership over the money in their pension accounts. Some may think of these ideas as liberal, others as conservative.

But most in **Since Sliced Bread** left that kind of categorization at the door. They were more concerned with what worked and which ideas could make America work better.

Fifth, Americans need to be included in a conversation about their nation's future. Once it was possible to make decisions in Washington or New York and expect people around the country to fall into line. That's not how it works anymore. And we are lucky that it doesn't. Because in idea after idea, ordinary Americans produced proposals with flashes of wisdom, insight, and inventiveness.

They thought so far outside the box that they called into question the basic assumptions of both political parties, but their ideas were very often practical, achievable with real political will behind them, and built on America's best values and the most noble episodes of our past.

S
ome of the ideas that were submitted really do have the potential to completely change the course of America for the better—others are interesting ideas that just wouldn't work for one reason or another. But when you look at them together, and read the words of deep passion with which they were submitted, a basic truth comes shining through: America needs to take a different direction if we are going to honor the work of our people and give them better lives—and those very same people have some ideas on how to do that which need to be heard and heeded.

Since Sliced Bread was not the end of that conversation. Rather, it was the beginning of the work we all need to do to put Americans into the driver's seat of our economic destiny. Most everywhere we look, Americans are seeking to make more decisions about their own lives.

Our "one-size-fits-all" world is being replaced with one of many options. People are no longer willing to let someone else—be it a doctor or travel agent or record company executive—make all their choices for them. But so far, the decisions and discussions about America's economic future have still been happening behind closed doors and with little input from the public at large.

The common-sense ideas that came through **Since Sliced Bread** were exciting and important, but if this contest is remembered for anything, I hope it is as a moment when Americans started to take the first steps toward becoming more active participants in the debates over where workers' lives are headed.

The 1.8 million workers of SEIU will be part of bringing that about. But we cannot do it alone.

Americans have to band together to shake our political system out of its stupor and make our voices and our ideas heard. That's the only way to really change America's direction and doing that—it seems to me—is the best idea since sliced bread.

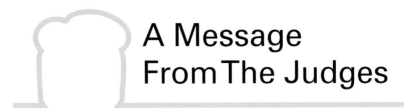

A Message From The Judges

There are few initiatives in America that would have brought the three of us—a former Democratic senator, Ronald Reagan's campaign manager, and the president of the largest African-American-owned mutual fund company in the world—together.

But when we were approached to participate as judges in **Since Sliced Bread**, we each enthusiastically agreed because we knew this was an important opportunity to capture the voices and ideas of people around America who are being left out of a Washington-centered political debate.

We knew ordinary Americans had good ideas but never anticipated the flood of ideas that came forward from thousands of Americans. Some of the ideas were revolutionary in their scope, others were just plain common sense. Some of the ideas were completely original, others have been talked about before but never truly tried. It was a chance for Americans to express their frustration with a political system that has not been reacting to the lives they live and to express their hopes for ways America could be made stronger and better.

The three of us were part of a group of 23 judges whose breadth of experience and commitment to a better America inspired us and is a testament to what an important role this contest played. The judges came from all around the country and across the ideological spectrum, from government and business and non-profits. They were CEOs and Pulitzer Prize-winning journalists. Academics and community organizers. Former leaders of the Environmental Protection Agency and U.S. Army and current leaders of the Sierra Club and Teach for America. (It's worth noting that while the Service Employees International Union created and financed **Since Sliced Bread**, its president—Andrew Stern—got only one vote as a judge, just like everyone else.)

The judges had a difficult job picking the final 21 ideas. There were hard choices, but we each cast our votes for our favorite ideas—and then put the final balloting in the hands of the members of the **Since Sliced Bread** community. Over 40,000 votes were cast. The winners are the first three ideas featured in this book.

Already, **Since Sliced Bread** ideas are having an impact. In 2006, Senator Hillary Rodham Clinton unveiled an idea to link Congressional pay raises to increases in the minimum wage—an idea related to one of our winning ideas and actually submitted by three members of the sinceslicedbread.com community. SEIU gave the **Since Sliced Bread** community the opportunity to ask their Senators to co-sponsor it and over 10,000 emails arrived in Senate inboxes. In Washington State a clean-energy ballot initiative passed that is closely related to the grand prize idea. SEIU joined with the environmental community in support of it and our winner, Peter Skidmore, was one of its principal spokespersons.

This is just the beginning. There is real potential for **Since Sliced Bread** to directly affect American families and to continue an extraordinary dialogue begun when the contest was launched.

We look forward to its future.

Sincerely,

Bill Bradley   **Mellody Hobson**   **Ed Rollins**

The Judges

Bill Bradley
Managing Director,
Allen & Company, LLC;
Former United States
Senator (D-NJ)

Lloyd H. Dean
President and CEO,
Catholic Healthcare West

Carol M. Browner
Principal,
The Albright Group, LLC;
Former Administrator,
U.S. Environmental
Protection Agency

Amy L. Domini
Founder and CEO,
Domini Social Invest-
ments, LLC;
President, Domini Social
Equity Fund

Louis E. Caldera
President,
University of New Mexico;
Former Secretary of
the Army

Esther Dyson
Editor-at-Large,
CNET Networks

Gail C. Christopher
Vice President,
Joint Center for Political
and Economic Studies,
Office of Health, Women
and Families

Jeff Faux
Founding President,
Distinguished Fellow,
Economic Policy Institute

Brian Dabson
Associate Director, Rural
Policy Research Institute;
Research Professor, Truman
School of Public Affairs,
University of Missouri

Bill Frenzel
Guest Scholar, Economic
Studies, The Brookings
Institution;
Former Member of
Congress (R-MN)

Mellody Hobson
President, Ariel Capital Management, Inc.

Carl Pope
Executive Director, The Sierra Club

Alan Khazei
Co-Founder and Chief Executive Officer, City Year, Inc.

Edward J. Rollins
Republican Political Commentator and Strategist

Donna Klein
President and CEO, Corporate Voices for Working Families

David K. Shipler
Pulitzer Prize-winning author: The Working Poor: Invisible in America

Charles E.M. Kolb
President, Committee for Economic Development; Former Deputy Assistant to President George H. W. Bush

David L. Sifry
Founder and CEO, Technorati

Wendy Kopp
President and Founder, Teach for America

Andrew L. Stern
International President, Service Employees International Union

Ginger Lew
CEO, Three Oaks, LLC

Kathryn Wylde
President and Chief Executive Officer, Partnership for New York City

Martha Phillips
Former Executive Director, The Concord Coalition

Judges' titles for identification only and represent positions held at the time of the contest.

1 Sustainable Resource Industries

Submitted by Peter Skidmore in Washington

Globalization of labor, production, and ideas and an industrial economy based on subsidized fossil fuels have set the stage for economic and social instability, continued outsourcing of jobs, and marginalized quality of life. We can create a new economy based on environmentally benign industries and energy.

We should impose a "resource tax" on pollution, development, and fossil fuels to pay for development of renewable energy and environmental restoration. Promoting sustainable localized energy industries (solar, wind, hydro, tidal, biofuels) will provide reliable, clean homegrown energy, exportable technologies, and bring energy jobs home. Funding widespread environmental restoration will expand existing industries (farming, recreation, tourism, and commercial fisheries) that are dependent on ecological services and will foster research, design, and technology industries.

Working families will benefit from a stable economy and millions of new economy jobs. These solutions are inherently local—they create decentralized resources and require skilled local labor, forever. They pay for themselves and provide capital for entrepreneurs to develop industries and exportable technologies. And they foster community and collaboration essential to surviving in a global economy.

Bio :: Peter Skidmore

Jocelyn Augustino

When a friend suggested a dinner with seven or eight others to discuss ideas for **Since Sliced Bread**, Peter Skidmore, 42, joined in because he enjoys "good intellectual discussions." He came away deciding to enter the contest to advocate sustainable resource industries that protect and restore the environment. "Right now we're spending our children's and our grandchildren's quality of life, not just their livelihoods," he says. "Let's start by fixing the damage we've caused." Skidmore is a geologist at the Nature Conservancy who develops priorities for freshwater conservation within Washington State. He earned his B.S. in geology from Macalester College and an M.S. in earth sciences from Montana State University. Skidmore lives in Seattle with his wife and two young sons. He's competed in the world championships (master's division) of ultimate frisbee.

Resources on a Sustainable Environment:

- The Nature Conservancy: http://www.nature.org
- Sierra Club: http://www.sierraclub.org/policy/conservation/taxes.asp
- "What in the World Are Green Taxes?" E/The Environmental Magazine: http://www.emagazine.com/view/?456
- Friends of the Earth: http://www.foe.org
- The Apollo Alliance: http://www.apolloalliance.org
- National Mining Association: http://www.nma.org
- Redefining Progress: http://www.rprogress.org
- World Wildlife Fund: http://www.worldwildlife.org
- Institute for Local Self-Reliance: http://www.ilsr.org

Facts :: Sustainable Environment

Economists estimate five million new jobs could be created if America embarked on a full-scale renewable energy program aimed at reducing drastically the 12 million barrels of oil the U.S. imports each day on average.[1]

The U.S. lags behind its global competitors in the critical green markets of the future while literally millions of jobs go abroad, according to the Apollo Alliance. Japan alone now controls 50% of the solar power market, an industry invented in America. European countries control 90% of wind turbine production. And the U.S. is importing fuel cells from Canada.[2]

The threat of global warming is escalating rapidly. The world is experiencing a rise in sea levels, the thawing of permafrost, and the acidification of the oceans. Higher temperatures threaten dangerous consequences, according to the Natural Resources Defense Council, such as drought, disease, floods, and lost eco-systems. Most heat-trapping gases come from power plants and vehicles.[3]

Solar power provides only 0.1% of the overall energy supply in the U.S. Fossil fuels, often cited for harmful emissions of pollutants, provide more than 85% of U.S. energy needs.[4]

Energy generated by wind power emits no air pollutants or greenhouse gases and is renewable. California's wind power plants offset the emission of more than 2.5 billion pounds of carbon dioxide, and 15 million pounds of other pollutants. It would take a forest of 175 million trees to provide the same air quality.[5]

America produces nearly a quarter of the world's greenhouse-gas emissions. China is expected to overtake the U.S. as the world's largest carbon emitter sometime around 2025.[6]

Investment in new renewable energy sources leads to roughly 10 times more jobs than a comparable investment in the fossil-fuel sector, according to Prof. Daniel Kammen, head of UC Berkeley's Renewable and Appropriate Energy Laboratory.[7]

The Superfund waste cleanup law passed in 1980, based on "the polluter pays," assessed a tax on firms that contaminate our air, water, and communities. The money went to a trust fund to pay for clean-ups at the worst industrial sites. In 2002 the polluter tax was rejected as "burdensome" to industry, so taxpayers now carry the burden and fewer Superfund sites are cleaned up.[8]

2 Tie Minimum Wage to Cost of Living

Submitted by Filippo Menczer in Indiana

Many of America's working poor earn minimum wage. As the cost of living increases, the purchasing power of the minimum wage goes down, and a political fight becomes necessary to raise the minimum wage every few years (or many, as in the current case).

This is unfair. A minimum should be a minimum in terms of purchasing power, not in inflation-bound dollars.

The solution is simple: Tie the minimum wage to the Cost-of-Living index.

This is fair, helps the neediest American working families, and saves Americans from a useless recurrent political fight.

Bio :: Filippo Menczer

Indexing the minimum wage to the cost of living is "the ethical thing to do," says Filippo Menczer, associate professor of computer science and informatics at Indiana University. "I'm very lucky. I have a good job and make a good living and I work hard. But there are people who work just as hard as me or much harder and they can't buy the food they need, pay their bills and make a living wage." Menczer, 41, came to the U.S. from Italy for graduate study in 1990. He's a specialist in artificial intelligence and web search engines. The IU professor notes that indexing the minimum wage has been advocated for years, in part because it's "simple social justice." Menczer and his wife, Colleen, plan to donate part of their contest award to charity. "This is a contest seeking to improve the lives of working people, so how could we do something selfish with it?" he asks.

Resources on the Minimum Wage:

- Economic Policy Institute:
  http://www.epi.org/content.cfm/webfeatures_snapshots_20051221
- ACORN Living Wage Campaign: http://www.livingwagecampaign.org
- Economic Opportunity Institute:
  http://www.econop.org/MinimumWage/MW-FAQs98.htm
- Center for Policy Alternatives:
  http://www.stateaction.org/issues/issue.cfm/issueLivingWage.xml
- "What Is a Living Wage?" By John Gertner, *New York Times Sunday Magazine*, January 15, 2006.
- Center for Economic and Policy Research: http://www.cepr.net

Real Value of Minimum Wage From 1997 to 2005, Washington State and the Nation[9]

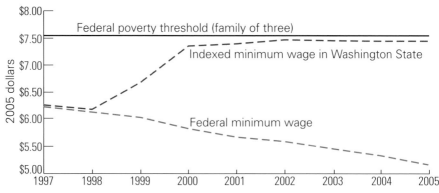

Facts :: Minimum Wage

The federal minimum wage—$5.15 per hour in 2006—is not indexed to inflation. A full-time minimum wage worker earned barely $10,000 per year, far below the $20,000 government experts say is needed for a family of four to live above the poverty level. Congress in early 2007 appeared close to adopting a minimum wage increase.[10]

Because the last increase in the federal minimum wage occurred in 1997, workers' purchasing power eroded as prices increased. Thus, the inflation-adjusted minimum wage was 20% less than when it last increased in 1997 and 30% lower today than in 1979. The federal minimum was 40% higher in 1968, or $8.50 in today's dollars.[11]

The failure of Congress to raise the federal minimum wage for years has led 19 states and the District of Columbia to enact minimum wage requirements higher than the federal level. The California minimum wage in 2006 was $6.75, Connecticut $7.65, and Washington $7.63.[12]

Some states, including Washington (1998), Oregon (2002), and Florida (2004), already link their state minimum wage levels to the cost of living. Vermont will do so in 2007. This inflation indexing guarantees low-wage workers a wage that goes up with the rising cost of goods and services.[13]

Some cities and counties also have enacted higher "living wage" levels that usually cover specific sets of workers, such as those employed by government or by businesses with government contracts or subsidies. Santa Fe, NM had a minimum wage of $9.50 an hour as of 2006.[14]

The Economic Policy Institute estimates that 14.9 million workers would benefit from a proposal to raise the federal minimum wage to $7.25 by 2008. Of those workers, 80% are adults and 59% are women. About 44% work full-time and another 34.5% work between 20 and 34 hours per week. The average minimum wage worker brings home about half of his or her family's weekly earnings.[15]

Employers, particularly restaurants and small businesses, argue that even modest increases in the minimum wage, including linking it to the cost of living, will result in job losses. But academic studies, such as one conducted by two Princeton economists, showed that a modest increase in the minimum wage did not cause any significant harm to employment, and indeed even resulted in a slight jobs increase.[16]

Indexing doesn't improve conditions for low-wage workers—it just keeps them from deteriorating further as prices rise, according to Prof. Robert Pollin.[17]

3 Reforming Public Education

Submitted by Leslie Hester in North Carolina

The future of American workers in the global economy depends on the quality and equity of today's public education. From kindergarten to college, our public institutions represent the capacity of our society to provide adequate income, health care, and security for all Americans. In this light, the following three reforms will return public education to its original mandate:

1. Restructure public funding of schools to redirect local property taxes to a general state fund that is then equitably distributed among all schools on a per-student basis. This measure would break the cycle of poverty endemic to those areas without a large property tax base.

2. Control tuition at public universities to better reflect the traditional statewide median income-to-cost of attendance ratio. This will provide all willing students the ability to receive a top-notch in-state education regardless of their families' economic status.

3. Increase teacher salaries to recruit and retain some of America's brightest. If we invest in high quality instruction, we give ourselves the best chance for an intelligent, entrepreneurial, and confident workforce.

Bio :: Leslie Hester

"Education is key to creating opportunities for working Americans," says Leslie Hester, a graduate student in the College of Natural Resources at North Carolina State University. Hester, who studies forestry, is a product of public schools, including the University of Georgia where she majored in ecology. "I'm concerned that when I have kids they may not be able to afford the tuition," she worries. Hester also sees a need for the U.S. to invest in better pay for K-12 teachers. "A number of my friends would have loved to teach, but the jobs came with a lot of stress and pay that was too low," she says. Hester, 27, enjoys playing blue-grass fiddle. She lives in Raleigh, NC with her husband, Barry. "I read about **Since Sliced Bread** in an online article and my husband and I started brainstorming that same night," she says.

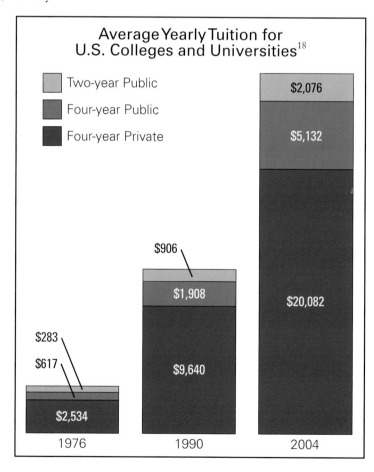

Average Yearly Tuition for U.S. Colleges and Universities[18]

Two-year Public
Four-year Public
Four-year Private

	1976	1990	2004
Two-year Public	$283	$906	$2,076
Four-year Public	$617	$1,908	$5,132
Four-year Private	$2,534	$9,640	$20,082

Facts :: Public Education Reform

Currently, the average funding gap between comparable rich and poor school districts in America is about 3:1, according to analyst Richard D. Vogel. In some cases, it goes to 13:1—and the gap is widening.[19]

Despite the presence of federal and state policies aimed at reducing enrollment disparities in higher education, low-income students and students of color remain under-represented in universities nationwide. At the most elite private colleges, three quarters of the students come from upper middle-class or wealthy families, according to Demos, a think tank. Only five percent come from families with household incomes under $35,000.[20]

A child from a family in the top income quartile is five times more likely to earn a bachelor's degree by age 24 than is a child from the bottom income quartile.[21]

The average Pell Grant now covers 25% of the total costs at public four-year colleges, down from 47% in 1975, and 10% of private college costs, down from 24% in 1975.[22]

In recent years, small annual increases in public school teachers' salaries have not been keeping pace with inflation. The average teacher salary in the 2003-04 school year was $46,597, a 2.2% increase from the year before, which fell short of the rate of inflation for 2004 (2.7%). Furthermore, many states are attempting to drastically reduce or eliminate teachers' pension and health care benefits.[23]

High school students living in low-income families drop out of school at six times the rate of their peers from high-income families.[24]

Resources on Public Education:

- National Education Association: http://www.nea.org
- American Federation of Teachers: http://www.aft.org
- Association of American Colleges and Universities: http://www.aacu.org
- Center for Education Policy and Leadership: http://www.education.umd.edu/EDPA/CEPAL
- *School: The Story of American Public Education.* PBS: http://www.pbs.org/kcet/publicschool/about_the_series/index.html
- Teachers Have It Easy: Big Sacrifices and Small Salaries of America's Teachers. By Dave Eggers, Ninive Clements Calegari and Daniel Moulthrop, 2005.
- The Teaching Commission: http://www.theteachingcommission.org

NURSE
STATION

4 Medicare as Single Payer Pilot Program

Submitted by Shannon Thomas in California

National health insurance is a controversial idea that has not been tested in America. The debate seems to get bogged down in fears of rationing and "socialized medicine." Wouldn't it be great if we could find a way to "try before you buy?"

Idea: Medicare Expansion Pilot Program. Give 10-20 of the nation's largest employers (including the federal government) the opportunity to use Medicare as their company's health insurance for five years.

The key difference would be they would pay premiums just like they would with a private insurer instead of the program being supported by taxes. Medicare's administrative costs are exponentially lower than most private insurers, which should result in significant savings.

Also invited into the program would be every resident of Washington, DC, regardless of employment status, to give a window on how insuring the uninsured would impact costs, service, etc.

This program would give us the opportunity to see the system in action, study it, and have real world evidence by which to evaluate the feasibility of national health insurance.

Bio :: Shannon Thomas

Shannon Thomas, 37, works as an executive assistant in the health care unit of the RAND Corporation. Her job helped Thomas see first-hand the shortcomings of America's current health care system. "You can't walk into a Taco Bell that hasn't got a letter grade from the health department on the wall, but you walk into a hospital and you don't have a clue how competent they are," she says. "A bad surgeon can kill you. A bad taco can't." Thomas grew up in the Bay Area and earned a B.A. from University of California-Berkeley after doing a thesis on poverty policy. She went on to Golden Gate Baptist Theological Seminary where she got a masters in music. After clicking on an Internet ad describing the **Since Sliced Bread** contest, she entered her proposal for a pilot project to use Medicare as a single payer health insurance program at 10 or 20 major corporations.

Resources on Medicare and Health Insurance:

- Medicare Rights Center: http://www.medicarerights.org
- Americans for Health Care: http://www.americansforhealthcare.org
- "Facts About Single Payer Health Insurance": http://www.pages.drexel.edu/~dar36/facts.html
- Physicians for a National Health Program: http://www.pnhp.org
- Healthcare-NOW!: http://www.healthcare-now.org
- Campaign for a National Health Program: http://www.cnhpnow.org
- "Paying More but Getting Less: Myths and the Global Case for U.S. Health Reform." By Tom Daschle, Center for American Progress, November 2005: http://www.americanprogress.org/
- Grahamazon: http://www.grahamazon.com/sp/whatissinglepayer.php

Health Care Spending as Percentage of GDP[25]

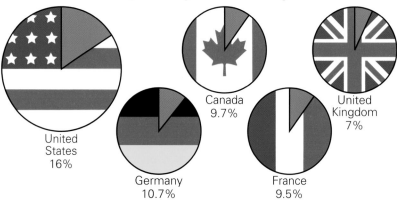

United States 16%

Canada 9.7%

United Kingdom 7%

Germany 10.7%

France 9.5%

Facts :: Medicare and Health Insurance

 Nearly two-thirds of Americans favor a government guarantee of health insurance for all—even if it means raising taxes, according to a 2005 survey by the Pew Research Center.[26]

Medicare, the government health insurance program, is far more efficient than private health care. Medicare has administrative costs of only about 2-3%. By contrast, private insurance plans, on average, spend about 9.5% of total costs for administration.[27]

 Medicare has proved to be more successful than private insurance in controlling the growth rate of health care spending per enrollee. Private insurers' costs grew 44% more than Medicare's from 1970 to 2000.[28]

More than 46 million people in the U.S. currently have no health insurance and millions more have inadequate coverage. About 8.3 million children have no health care. One-third of U.S. expenditures are a result of excessive administrative costs and escalating profits for private corporations.[29]

 The U.S. ranks 37th among the countries of the world in the provision of health care, according to the World Health Organization. Americans have a shorter life expectancy and can expect to die younger than citizens of 34 other nations, including Cyprus and Singapore. And the U.S. has higher infant mortality than that of 41 other countries, including Slovenia and South Korea.[30]

A study by researchers at Harvard Medical School found that national health insurance could save at least $286 billion annually on paperwork—enough to cover all of the uninsured. The authors found that bureaucracy accounts for at least 31% of total U.S. health spending compared to 16.7% in Canada, which has a government health program.[31]

Nearly 33% of Hispanics living in the U.S. are uninsured—about 14.1 million total. Many are in working families. About 20% of African-Americans are uninsured, compared to 11% of whites.[32]

Since Medicare began in 1965, poverty among the elderly has been reduced by nearly two-thirds.[33]

5 Help Working Families Save More

Submitted by Christopher Wimer in Massachusetts

The Earned Income Tax Credit (EITC) is one of the most successful poverty-reduction programs in recent years. Yet working families continue to face increasing uncertainty with the volatile job market of the new economy and the tenuous future of bedrock social insurance programs, such as Social Security.

By making it easier for EITC beneficiaries to channel a portion of their benefits into savings accounts, we could provide the beginnings of a support system for America's insecure workforce.

EITC beneficiaries could be provided with savings options when they claim their EITC on their annual tax forms. Portions of EITC payments could be put into Individual Development Accounts, in which the government matches deposits that will be channeled to ends like education, starting a business, or purchasing a home.

Alternatively, EITC payments could be put into tax-exempt investments so that low- and moderate-income working parents could begin to save for their futures and their families.

Bio :: Christopher Wimer

Chris Wimer, 29, is a Ph.D student in the Sociology and Social Policy program at Harvard. He's active in a new student-run think tank called the New Vision Institute (www.newvisioninstitute.org) and learned about **Since Sliced Bread** from a fellow policy wonk there. "At New Vision there are young and established scholars interested in politically relevant policy work," Wimer says. He and four others there developed contest ideas and gave each other feedback. The Earned Income Tax Credit is based on the concept that "if you work, you shouldn't be poor," Wimer says, "and there's evidence that, if you give people easy options to save, they'll actually do so." Wimer loves to play tennis, follows the Boston Red Sox, and belongs to a restaurant group that tries out a new eatery each month. He volunteers in an after-school program run mainly by Harvard undergraduates who provide homework help and academic enrichment to students in two housing projects in Boston's Mission Hill.

Resources on the Earned Income Tax Credit:

- Center on Budget and Policy Priorities:
  http://www.cbpp.org/pubs/eitc.htm
- Wikipedia: http://en.wikipedia.org/wiki/Earned_income_tax_credit
- Citizens for Tax Justice: http://www.ctj.org
- Clinton Foundation EITC Resource Center:
  http://www.clintonfoundation.org/cf-pgm-ee-eitc.htm
- Democratic Leadership Council:
  http://www.dlc.org/ndol_ci.cfm?kaid=139&subid=277&contentid=3607
- Economic Policy Institute:
  http://www.epinet.org/content.cfm/briefingpapers_eitc

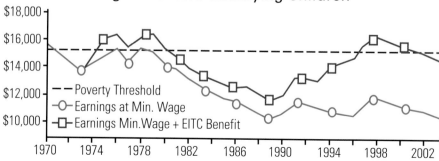

Income for Full-Time Worker at Minimum Wage, Single With Two Qualifying Children[34]

Facts :: Earned Income Tax Credit

The Earned Income Tax Credit, or EITC, reduces tax burdens and supplements wages for low-income working families. Those with children who have annual incomes below about $37,000 generally are eligible. In 2003, the average EITC was $2,100. Workers who have incomes below about $12,000 and don't have children can receive a very small EITC.[35]

The EITC is a "refundable" tax credit, which means that if a worker's income tax liability is less than the amount of the credit for which he or she qualifies, the worker receives the remaining amount of the credit as a refund. The EITC was fashioned in part to offset the regressive payroll tax burdens that low-income workers face, as well as income taxes that they may owe.[36]

A key goal of the EITC is to "make work pay"—rewarding work by reducing the taxes that low-wage workers pay on their earnings and by supplementing their wages. The program seeks to bring a family with a full-time minimum-wage worker up to the poverty line.[37]

Ronald Reagan, George H. W. Bush, and Bill Clinton all praised the EITC and proposed expansions of it. The reason: the EITC has produced substantial increases in employment and large decreases in poverty. It has enjoyed bipartisan support since it began in 1975.[38]

About 75% of the EITC benefits go to families with adjusted gross incomes between $5,000 and $20,000 a year. Some 31% of the benefits went to those with incomes between $10,000 and $15,000, while 21% went to those earning from $5,000 to $10,000 a year.[39]

Economists and politicians have proposed improvements to the EITC, including expanding the benefit for families with three or more children and increasing dramatically the EITC benefits for low-income workers who are not raising minor children.[40]

Nineteen states have enacted tax credits for low- and moderate-income working families based on the federal Earned Income Tax Credit. A number of additional states took up the issue in 2006. A substantial portion of those who file for the federal credit fail to claim the additional state credit, often because they are unaware the state EITC program exists.[41]

In 2003, the EITC directly lifted 2.4 million children in working families above the poverty line. Census data show that 4.4 million people rose out of poverty that year due to the program.[42]

6 Create National Farm Produce Network

Submitted by Kate Ward in Illinois

Creating a national produce distribution network addresses health, labor justice, and unequal government spending. The government's farm subsidies mostly go to a few huge corporate farmers, and stores in poor neighborhoods struggle to get quality, affordable fruits and vegetables.

Instead of enriching big agribusinesses with our tax dollars, use farm subsidies to build a nationwide produce distribution network. This will help small farmers market their produce widely and resist being absorbed by huge conglomerates. Better, cheaper fruits and vegetables everywhere will help Americans fight obesity and related diseases, which will improve quality of life and job productivity and cut down on government and personal health care spending. Strengthen the market for American soybeans by running the distribution trucks on clean, domestically produced biodiesel.

Finally, farms that receive grants must undergo a yearly audit of labor and environmental practices. Standards should be set by a panel that includes farmworkers and environmental advocates.

Bio :: Kate Ward

Kate Ward, 24, is a student at Catholic Theological Union in Chicago. She grew up near Albany, New York and earned an A.B. in psychology from Harvard. "Living in the city, the produce you can get is often dicey," she says. "We need to find ways for small farmers to get their fruits and vegetables to urban markets as part of helping people live healthier lives." She wants to divert some of the big subsidies now going to huge agribusinesses to family farmers and to a distribution network for them. Ward enjoyed South Asian dance at Harvard and helped lead the Catholic Student Association there. She did her senior thesis on "people's implicit perception of God's gender." Ward enjoys reading fiction (The Alchemist and Carter Beats the Devil are two favorites) and found the film *Brokeback Mountain* "really moving."

Resources on Agriculture Policy:

- The Agribusiness Accountability Initiative: http://www.agribusinessaccountability.org/
- Farm Worker Justice Fund: http://www.fwjustice.org/
- United Farm Workers: http://www.ufw.org/
- National Biodiesel Board: http://www.biodiesel.org/
- Think Fresh! Partnerships for Promotion of Vegetables and Fruits in Low-Income Communities (Broadcast available through the Public Health Foundation): http://bookstore.phf.org/prod344.htm

Farm and Other Commercial Land Use in the U.S.[43]

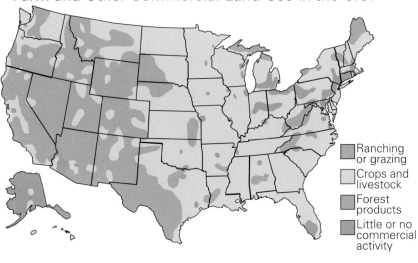

Ranching or grazing

Crops and livestock

Forest products

Little or no commercial activity

Facts :: Agriculture Policy

 High prices for quality fruits and vegetables may lead to increased weight gain in school-age children, particularly those who live in low-income areas.[44] Recent figures from the Centers for Disease Control and Prevention indicate that approximately 130 million Americans are either overweight or obese, costing the nation an estimated $117 billion in direct medical costs and indirect costs, such as lost wages due to illness.[45]

The world's wealthiest countries spend approximately $1 billion a day on domestic agricultural subsidies—more than six times what they spend on overseas aid each year.[46] The U.S. Farm Bill passed in 2002 provides for $190 billion in assistance to the American agricultural sector over the decade to follow.[47]

 The primary beneficiaries of U.S. agricultural subsidies have shifted dramatically with the changing face of American agriculture. When federal subsidies were first mandated in the 1930s, approximately a quarter of the U.S. population resided on the nation's six million small farms. Six decades later, 72% of farm sales were accounted for by 157,000 large farms, and 2% of Americans resided on farms.[48]

Far from serving as a safety net for poor farmers, farm subsidies now constitute America's largest corporate welfare program, according to many economists. Both the conservative Heritage Foundation and the liberal Environmental Working Group argue that the flow of farm subsidies has never been more biased in favor of large agribusiness operations than it has in recent years, due to the controversial "freedom to farm" policies introduced in 1996. In recent years, 10% of the highest-paid recipients collected more than 61% of subsidies nationwide, with even larger disparities in Southern states.[49]

 American agribusiness relies heavily upon the cheap and seasonally-replaceable labor of approximately 3 million workers—many of whom are undocumented immigrants, women, and children. Because of exemptions in the Fair Labor Standards Act (FLSA), as well as weak enforcement of existing regulations, more than 100,000 child farmworkers in the United States currently work under dangerous and exhausting conditions, often suffering pesticide poisonings, heat-related illness, machine and knife-related injuries, and life-long disabilities.[50]

Biodiesel is a clean-burning alternative fuel produced from domestic, renewable resources. It is four times as efficient as diesel fuel in utilizing fossil energy, and its use in a conventional diesel engine results in a substantial reduction of unburned hydrocarbons, carbon monoxide, and particulate matter compared with emissions from diesel fuel.[51]

7 Protect Workers' Retirement Assets

Submitted by John Biddle in Florida

Problem: Workers need protection for their employer-funded retirement assets earned while they worked. Companies use long vesting periods to minimize the number of employees covered. Some underfund their pension funds and others go bankrupt, causing significant financial loss to their employees related to retirement.

Idea: Pass a law that requires companies to allocate their retirement funding dollars into approved individual retirement accounts for employees who choose that option. Also require that companies funding retirement benefits for their employees cannot discriminate against new employees through vesting policies. This would not mandate a retirement benefit, just require optional individual control over it.

Benefit: Hard-earned retirement assets would belong to workers, and would be protected against underfunding, fraud, and bankruptcy by their employer(s). Workers would be able to accumulate a full retirement nest egg even if they change jobs many times during their careers. Lastly, since the retirement asset is theirs, they can will it to whomever they choose.

RETIREMENT ASSETS

Bio :: John Biddle

For 13 years, John Biddle was a computer analyst at JPMorgan Chase & Co., the global financial services firm. His idea of developing strategies through which workers gain control of their retirement assets has a special resonance: Biddle retired after learning in 2006 that he would be laid off in a corporate downsizing. Biddle's watched as companies, such as airlines, have shed their underfunded pensions through bankruptcy, leaving workers with far-reduced benefits. "Nobody goes to jail," he says. "There's no punishment—it's called business, but it should be illegal." Biddle is married with two daughters and three grandchildren, lives in Clearwater, Florida, and holds an MBA in finance from University of South Florida. He and his wife enjoy kayaking on Florida rivers and like to travel to U.S. national parks. A self-described political "libertarian," Biddle wants wider pension options for individuals, but dismisses talk of an ownership society by President Bush as a "big mistake."

Resources on Retirement Security:

- Pension Rights Center: http://www.pensionrights.org
- Labor Research Association:
  http://www.laborresearch.org/story.php?id=407
- "Protect Your Pension." U.S. Department of Labor:
  http://www.dol.gov/ebsa/publications/protect_your_pension.html
- Pension Information and Counseling Projects:
  http://www.pensionrights.org/pages/help.html
- Economic Policy Institute:
  http://www.epi.org/content.cfm/issueguides_retirement_security
- Alliance for Retired Americans:
  http://www.retiredamericans.org
- Center for Retirement Research–Boston College:
  http://www.bc.edu/centers/crr/

READ ALL THE IDEAS ONLINE AT

SinceSlicedBread.com

Facts :: Retirement

Some workers and retirees at Enron, WorldCom, Global Crossing and other companies have seen their retirement security evaporate. Hoping their 401(k) money in their companies' stock would provide a decent retirement, too many Americans have been left with little but lawsuits and tears. The Pension Rights Center has a series of reforms called the 401(k) Action Initiative to prevent such debacles by limiting over-concentration of employer stock in 401(k) plans.[52]

Employers too often now fail to live up to their pension promises. Airline and steel workers who thought they had secure pensions later saw their companies shed those obligations easily in bankruptcy proceedings—leaving those workers with far smaller retirement incomes. The collapse of corporations too often costs not only jobs, but also the retirement income of workers. The government agency that insures traditional pension benefits estimates that defined benefit plans are underfunded by some $450 billion.[53]

Experts predict that most people are going to arrive at retirement without adequate money. Alicia Munnell of Boston College estimates that the bottom one-third of future retirees will be poor—far greater than today's 9.8% poverty rate for retirees. The middle third of future retirees will scrape by, if they have no big extra expenses. And the top third will be OK, Munnell predicts, yet many will be disappointed with their living standard.[54]

Retirement security often is described as a three-legged stool with the legs being Social Security, pensions, and savings. Social Security, despite claims by those who want to privatize it, won't be going broke—the trust fund is solvent for another 38 to 48 years if we do nothing. But the pension and savings legs are weakening.[55]

The U.S. pension system has two primary types of plans: defined benefit and defined contribution. With defined benefit plans, employers provide workers with a guaranteed level of retirement income normally based on years of service and pay level. With defined contribution plans, such as 401(k)s, employers and workers contribute to individual accounts with benefits dependent on investment outcome.[56]

About 34 million workers were covered in 2005 by defined-benefit pension plans. That was only a quarter of the U.S. workforce. As more families are covered by defined-contribution plans, the investment risk shifts from employers to employees.[57]

Workers contribute two of every three dollars to today's 401(k) defined contribution plans. About 20-30% of people eligible to participate in 401(k) plans don't contribute—many because they can't afford it.[58]

RETIREMENT ASSETS

8 Massive Public Works Projects

Submitted by Andrew Kosyjana in Maryland

Public works projects such as the Panama Canal, Hoover Dam, the Tennessee Valley Authority, and the New York City Water Tunnels have created infrastructure expansion, jobs, economic growth, and health care for millions of Americans.

In order to benefit Americans, I propose we initate massive public works projects, aimed at employment of Americans, economic growth, health care opportunities, and infrastructure expansion. Such projects would include re-opening steel mills, building hydroelectric plants or green-energy facilities, shipyards, bridges, roads, high-rise buildings, tunnels, and renovating existing towns and cities. When government, business, and industry start public works projects, every business has a chance to capitalize on the increase of productivity.

Another concept would be to start pilot towns that are built around the latest technologies, such as hybrid and zero-emission vehicles, broadband communications, renewable energy sources, mass-transit systems, and other emerging technologies that need to be tested full scale. This is a common-sense idea—even the Pharoahs and Emperors of ancient civilizations knew that if you keep your citizens employed and working, your economy will thrive.

Bio :: Andrew Kosyjana

Andrew Kosyjana, 25, trained as a chef. He works as a manager in the seafood department of a grocery chain. He worries about those in the greater Baltimore area who have lost jobs at steel mills and auto plants as work gets outsourced to Asia, Mexico, and elsewhere. His proposal for massive public works projects aims to expand employment and create economic growth here in the U.S. "Public works projects helped get us out of the Depression and, even though things aren't that bad today, we still need to drive our economy to create more jobs," Kosyjana says. He earned his associate degree in professional cooking from Baltimore International College. An avid reader interested in World War II history, Kosyjana likes to go out to clubs, "but I'm not known as a party person." He read about the **Sliced Bread** contest in *Parade* magazine and for many weeks went regularly to the website to submit ideas and comment on others' submissions.

Resources on Expanding Public Works:

- American Public Works Association: http://www.apwa.net
- National Construction Alliance: http://www.liuna.org
- Economic Policy Institute: http://www.epi.org
- American Society of Civil Engineers: http://www.asce.org
- Apollo Alliance: http://www.apolloalliance.org

Charles C. Ebbets

Facts :: Public Works Projects

 The top 10 public works projects of the 20th century: Panama Canal, Tennessee Valley Project, Hoover Dam, Bay Area Rapid Transit (BART), Grand Coulee Dam, Hyperion Treatment Plant, St. Lawrence Seaway, Interstate Highway System, Reversal of the Chicago River, and Golden Gate Bridge. These were selected by the American Public Works Association.[59]

Infrastructure failures in the U.S. occur every day. Most disastrous in the recent past has been the breaching of levees in New Orleans when Hurricane Katrina hit. Levees also failed in northern California during winter rainstorms in early 2006. And the breach of the Tam Sauk Reservoir in Missouri further underscored the need for public works funding to head off more such infrastructure failures.[60]

 Advocates of a huge public works effort on behalf of energy independence say it could create three million new jobs, free the nation from dependence on imported oil, and promote a healthier environment. The Apollo Alliance has called for a crash program to capture the green markets of the future through public support of renewable energy sources, such as windpower, biomass, and solar power.[61]

America's schools remain in need of massive modernization. Every school day, an estimated 14 million children attend schools in which the roofs leak, ventilation is poor, heating and air conditioning don't maintain reasonable temperatures, lighting is inadequate, and plumbing doesn't work. Instead of technologically cutting-edge schools that would prepare U.S. students for the global economy of the 21st century, the American Society of Civil Engineers gave a grade of "D" to U.S. schools.[62]

 U.S. building trades' unions advocate public works projects based on "best value contracting." The practice is endorsed by the U.S. Army Corps of Engineers and already is used in 70% of all federal projects. It's based on higher standards in the construction industry and no longer would reward "low bid" contracts by contractors who don't contribute to workers' health insurance, training, or pensions.[63]

Public investment often makes America more productive in the future and complements private investments. The large tax cuts for the wealthiest Americans in the last five years have drained the revenues that could be used for improving our declining infrastructure. Former Labor Secretary Robert Reich notes that our failure to invest adequately on essentials like mass transit and highways will hurt us in the decades ahead.[64]

9 A Flat Tax to Save Social Security

Submitted by David Cochran in Iowa

Working Americans deserve financially secure retirements, and Social Security helps make this possible. But eventually its payroll tax won't be able to cover its costs, and at precisely the time we need to respond by fixing Social Security, many conservatives are attacking it.

The irony is that the very concept these same conservatives usually support is exactly the thing to save Social Security: a flat tax. Social Security is funded by a 6.2% tax on wages up to $97,500 (in 2007). Everyone making under that pays the full amount, while those making more pay less. It is a regressive tax; the rich pay less, and the richer you are the less you pay.

The solution? Make the Social Security payroll tax flat. Everyone pays the same percentage of their income to support it. This simple fix will bring in enough to fully fund Social Security indefinitely. So those who praise the idea of a flat tax should put their money where their mouths are and support one that can save retirement security for working Americans!

Bio :: David Cochran

David Cochran, 38, teaches political philosophy and American government at Loras College in Dubuque, Iowa. His proposal for a "flat tax" to save Social Security grew out of classroom discussions in which his students expressed doubts that the program will be there when they retire. Under Cochran's plan, people who earn more than $97,500 a year would pay more into Social Security, as would employers. Those who earn less would not be affected by the change. "Most flax-tax advocates don't like progressive taxation and don't want their approach applied to Social Security," Cochran says. He grew up in Lubbock, Texas, went to Drew University, and earned his Ph.D in political science at University of Maryland. Married with two boys, ages 5 and 7, Cochran is a movie buff who enjoyed *The Constant Gardener*.

Resources on Social Security:

- Campaign for America's Future: http://socialsecurity.ourfuture.org
- Americans United to Protect Social Security:
  http://www.americansforsocialsecurity.com/
- "Social Security Issue Guide." Economic Policy Institute:
  http://www.epi.org/content.cfm/issueguide_socialsecurity
- "Lift the Cap on Social Security Taxes." By John Miller, *Monthly Review*,
  July 16, 2005: http://mrzine.monthlyreview.org/miller160705.html
- Center on Budget and Policy Priorities:
  http://www.cbpp.org/8-11-05socsec.htm
- Center for Economic and Policy Research:
  http://www.cepr.net/pages/socialsecuritymedicare.htm

Facts :: Social Security

 Social Security taxes fall most heavily on working people and the poor, rather than on those with high incomes. Those taxes are 6.2% on workers and 6.2% on employers—for a total of 12.4%.[65]

Social Security taxes are levied only on wage income and not other forms of income, such as stock dividends or real estate profits. There is a cap on wages subject to the tax, which was set at $97,500 in 2007 (the exact level rises slightly each year indexed to inflation). Pay above that level is not subject to the Social Security tax. Thus someone earning $1 million a year pays the same amount in Social Security taxes as someone making $97,500.[66]

 A *Washington Post* poll in February 2005 reported that 81% of respondents agreed that Americans should pay Social Security taxes on wages over the cap ($90,000 in 2005). A CNN/*USAToday*/Gallup poll that same month found two-thirds of Americans supported applying a Social Security tax on all income.[67]

The "flat tax" on Social Security—making everyone pay the same percentage on their entire wage income—would result in a change for about five percent of wage earners. This high-income group already has benefited from three rounds of tax cuts under President Bush.[68]

 The Social Security Administration in 2003 found that lifting the cap on wages/salaries would enable the trust fund to pay Social Security benefits through the year 2075, even if the high earners also receive larger benefits to reflect the extra money they pay in.[69]

President George W. Bush said during the 2005 debates over Social Security and private accounts that he would consider raising the cap, but would oppose raising payroll tax rates. Other opponents claim lifting the cap might discourage businesses from hiring additional workers.[70]

SOCIAL SECURITY FLAT TAX

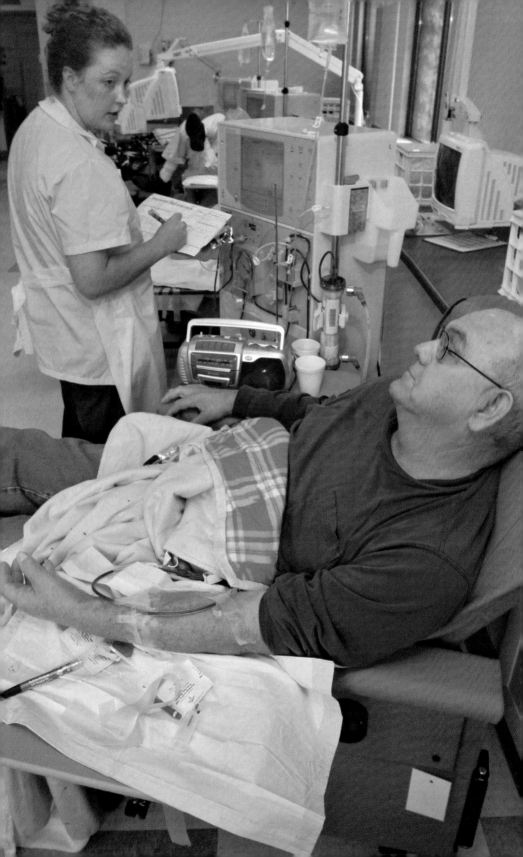

10 Three Steps to Universal Health Care

Submitted by Martin Johnson in North Carolina

A simple, slow, politically feasible way to provide for full national health care in 30 years:

1. Digital records: Invest in technology so we reduce waste in the system spent on paperwork. Also this has the advantage of creating the idea that it's one big health system, not many small systems. The concept is popular with Republicans and Democrats alike, so this should be easy.

2. Health care for children and young adults: Start a single-payer system, similar to Medicare, for everyone under the age of 35. Many young adults don't have health care, which puts them in danger and makes it more expensive for everyone else. By requiring children and young adults to have health care, costs will be controlled. Also, everyone can supplement their basic health care if they wish, and others can buy in.

3. With each passing year, people stay in the single-payer system. So, in 30 years time, everyone will have health care. This gradual system, like Social Security, will make health care what it should be: a right.

Bio :: Martin Johnson

Martin Johnson, 27, is a student who scrambles to get health care insurance coverage each time he moves up the academic ladder. After following the debate over Social Security financing, he concluded that political leaders need to face up to a bigger crisis: the need for single-payer universal health care. A political pragmatist, Johnson sees a need to start with digital health records—an idea both the right and left embrace. He'd then move on to establish a single-payer system like Medicare for everyone under age 35. They would stay in the system so that, with each passing year, more and more Americans would be covered. "It's difficult to go from where we are now to where we need to be," Johnson says. He received an undergraduate degree from Brown University and a masters in folklore from University of North Carolina. Johnson worked as a volunteer for John Edwards' presidential campaign in 2004.

Resources on National Health Insurance:

- Physicians for a National Health Program: http://www.pnhp.org
- Critical Condition: How Health Care in America Became Big Business—and Bad Medicine. By Donald Bartlett and James B. Steele. Doubleday, 2004.
- Publicly Funded Medicine: http://en.wikipedia.org/wiki/Publicly_funded_medicine
- One Nation Uninsured: Why the U.S. Has No National Health Insurance. By Jill Quadagno. Oxford University Press, 2005.
- Universal Health Care Action Network: http://www.uhcan.org
- "Who Should Pay for Health Care?" *The News Hour*, PBS: http://www.pbs.org/newshour/extra/features/jan-june04/uninsured_1-19.html
- "Universal Health Coverage: Coming Sooner Than You Think." By Leif Wellington Haase. The Century Foundation, 2005: http://www.tcf.org/list.asp?type=NC&pubid=1033
- "Crib Sheet: Universal Health Care—Debunking Five of the Right's Favorite Myths." By Tyler Zimmer, Campus Progress: http://www.campusprogress.org/tools/716/crib-sheet-universal-healthcare
- Insuring America's Health. Institute of Medicine, The National Academies, 2004: http://www.nationalacademies.org/news.nsf/isbn0309091055?OpenDocument

Facts :: National Health Insurance

 More than 46 million Americans, 15.9% of the population, are without health insurance. The uninsured receive less preventive care, are diagnosed at more advanced disease stages, and have higher mortality rates than insured individuals, reports the Institute of Medicine.[71]

 More than 13 million young adults ages 19 to 29 lacked health insurance in 2004. About 30% of 19 to 29-year-olds are uninsured, nearly double the rate for working-age adults over 30, according to a study by The Commonwealth Fund.[72]

The Bush Administration in 2004 released a proposal for every U.S. citizen's health information to be stored in an "electronic health record" database by 2014. This would be a digital file containing data on a person's medical history, allergies, insurance coverage, conditions such as asthma or diabetes, and prescription record.[73]

The number of uninsured children in 2005 was 8.3 million. More than 2 million children become uninsured each year after their parents lose their employer-based health insurance, according to the American Academy of Pediatrics.[74]

In 2004, the U.S. spent 16% of its Gross Domestic Product (GDP) on health care, estimated to rise to 18.7% in ten years. By contrast, health care spending was 10.7% of GDP in Germany, 9.7% in Canada, and 9.5% in France—all countries with national health care.[75]

The U.S. spends nearly $100 billion per year to provide uninsured residents with health services, often for preventable diseases, according to the Institute of Medicine.[76]

A single-payer national health insurance program could save approximately $150 billion annually on paperwork alone, says the Physicians for a National Health Program. About 25 percent of every health care dollar now goes to marketing, billing, utilization review, and other forms of administration.[77]

Percentage of Children Under Age 18 Without Health Insurance, 1987-2005[78]

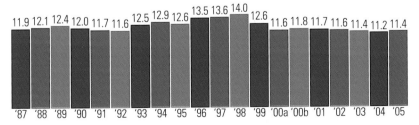

'87	'88	'89	'90	'91	'92	'93	'94	'95	'96	'97	'98	'99	'00a	'00b	'01	'02	'03	'04	'05
11.9	12.1	12.4	12.0	11.7	11.6	12.5	12.9	12.6	13.5	13.6	14.0	12.6	11.6	11.8	11.7	11.6	11.4	11.2	11.4

11 Create a "Civil Works Corps"

Submitted by Major Danny Clark in Florida

The U.S. government should consider creating a 50,000-strong Department of Defense-sponsored "Civil Works Corps" (CWC) similar to the New Deal era's Civilian Conservation Corps. Allocate a portion to each state or FEMA region and allow the National Guard's State Area Commands to manage their CWCs.

The CWCs would provide their region with valuable public works, such as national and public park maintenance, forestry (maintenance and fire-fighting), conservation management (erosion control projects), disaster response and recovery operations, public infrastructure improvement projects, security augmentation (albeit limited), and administrative support to state and local governments. Youths would "enlist" in the CWC for two to four years, earning 30 days of annual leave and medical benefits during the period. Honorably-discharged CWC "veterans" would earn college tuition assistance (one year paid per one year served) similar to the GI Bill.

The CWC would provide long-term investment in America's communities and help restore a sense of "collective duty to the greater good" to Americans that many older citizens who served in their youth contend is necessary for long-term cultural health and survival.

Bio :: Major Danny Clark

Major Danny Clark, who served with the Third U.S. Army in the first Gulf War, believes the military's role is to fight wars abroad and to protect us at home, but not "to fight fires in Colorado or wherever." He proposes a Civil Works Corps made up of young volunteers under command of the National Guard that would fight fires, perform conservation management, park maintenance, disaster response, and similar tasks. Clark grew up in Lawrence County, Tennessee where "my granddaddy was a school teacher and local politician who introduced me to Ronald Reagan." Clark earned a doctorate in education from University of Alabama and remains a staunch Crimson Tide football fan. After 27 years in the military, he is currently Deputy Provost Marshal for the U.S. Army Reserve Medical Command in Largo, Florida. He read about the contest in *Parade* magazine and entered seven ideas. Clark plans to keep advocating his Civil Works Corps proposal and wants to submit an article on it to a publication of the Reserve Officers' Association. He entertains his two children, ages 8 and 3, by "doing voices" imitating Yoda of *Star Wars* and also former Presidents Clinton and Reagan.

Facts :: Civil Works Corps

Officially termed the Emergency Conservation Work Act and affectionately known as "Roosevelt's Tree Army," the Civilian Conservation Corps was established by the executive order of President Franklin Delano Roosevelt on March 31, 1933—less than a month after his inauguration. The CCC fought both soil erosion and massive unemployment, dispatching jobless young people from large urban areas to revitalize the nation's decimated forests by planting an estimated three billion trees.[79]

In 1976—thirty-two years after the original CCC program disbanded—then-Governor Jerry Brown of California established the California Conservation Corps. This program differed drastically from the original CCC, primarily targeting youth development instead of economic revival. Today it is the largest, oldest, and longest-running youth conservation program in the world.[80]

The California Conservation Corps and other state and local models provide compelling archetypes that could be expanded on a national scale. One study found that youth conservation corps generate $1.60 in immediate benefits for every $1.00 in costs. Additionally, it was documented that participation in conservation corps programs provided an effective, long-term alternative to youth unemployment, incarceration, and substance abuse; enrollees had an arrest rate that was nearly one-third lower than their non-enrolled counterparts.[81]

Although the U.S. economy has gained jobs over the past decade, the number of unemployed youth in America has been steadily rising. This is particularly true for African-American youth between the ages of 16 and 24, whose unemployment rate is nearly seven times the overall national rate.[82]

According to the International Labor Organization, youth unemployment has skyrocketed worldwide over the past decade to some 88 million, reaching an all-time high with young people aged 15 to 24 now representing nearly half the world's jobless.[83]

Resources on the Civil Works Corps:

- The National Association of Service and Conservation Corps:
  http://www.nascc.org
- *Global Employment Trends for Youth, 2004.* International Labour Office,
  Geneva, 2004. ISBN 92-2-115997-3: http://www.ilo.org/trends
- History of the Civilian Conservation Corps:
  http://www.cccalumni.org/history1.html

12 Blanket the U.S. With Wireless Internet

Submitted by Michael Kunitzky in New Jersey

Information is too restricted and not accessible enough to most people. The barriers to obtaining information (one being cost) are creating a huge separation of the "information haves" and the "information have-nots." The gap will continue to widen unless/until there is a big enough change to shift the balance.

We should implement widespread WiFi / WiMax networks across as many cities as possible. Provide free (or VERY low cost) wireless broadband Internet access to all U.S. citizens, so that everyone has equal access to the information, and more importantly to the technology revolution that is continuing to re-shape the world. By leaving certain citizens, particularly children, without broadband Internet access, we are handicapping those people for life. It's a fast-changing world, and we have to help everyone keep up.

Providing wireless broadband access to all citizens will be the first, and biggest, step toward leveling the playing field of the classes. Not only will the increased access help lift lower classes, it will spur new technology developments and initiatives that will touch everyone.

Bio :: Michael Kunitzky

Michael Kunitzky, 32, lives in Brooklyn, New York where he works in corporate development for an interactive marketing and technology company. He studied engineering at University of Buffalo and earned a degree in forensic psychology from John Jay College. Kunitzky's brother forwarded him a link to **SinceSlicedBread.com** just hours before the contest ended. "I've worried that there's a divide that falls along socio-economic lines here and throughout the world between those who can afford broadband Internet access and those who can't," Kunitzky says. Universal access to high-speed Internet is feasible both technically and economically, he believes, but the problem is "opposition from the big telecom firms." When he's not hiking or mountain biking in the Adirondacks, Kunitzky enjoys photography and has a blog at www.alwayslookaround.com. "My plan may not be the most unique of ideas, but people don't realize just how possible it is," Kunitzky says.

Internet Access, 2000-2005[84]

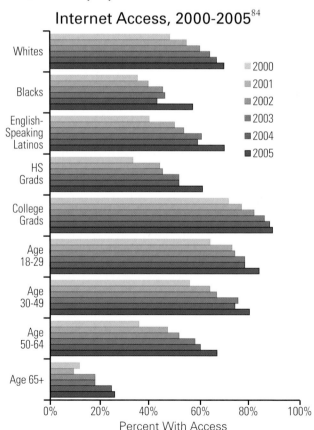

Facts :: Internet Access

 Cities across the country—from San Francisco to Philadelphia—are experimenting with providing free or low-cost wireless access to underserved neighborhoods. Supporters of these initiatives argue that the digital airwaves are a public entity that—like water or mail delivery—should be accessible to all citizens. Law enforcement, businesses, and an array of government offices are also likely to benefit from area-wide WiFi networks.[88]

Although more than 137 million Americans used the Internet in 2005, an increase of five percentage points from the previous year, there are still countless low-income families that have been left behind by the technological revolution.[85]

 Race and education are also significant variables in determining techno-haves and have-nots. Fifty-seven percent of African-Americans have online access, compared with 70% of whites. Twenty-nine percent of those who have not graduated from high school have access, compared with 61% of high school graduates and 89% of college graduates, according to the Pew Internet Project.[86]

The digital divide is even more drastic in the developed world: the 942 million people living in the world's developed economies enjoy nine times better access to Internet services and own 13 times more PCs than the 85% of the world's population living in low- and lower-middle income countries.[87]

 Telecommunications companies protest that government-funded WiFi initiatives impede upon the rights of private enterprise at high capital and efficiency costs for the public. In several states, cable companies have successfully lobbied to prohibit or restrict the networks claiming they constitute unfair, taxpayer-funded competition.[89]

The Pew Internet Project reports that adults in households with annual incomes of $30,000 or less are about half as likely as the highest-income Americans to go online. About 93% of highest-income Americans have Internet access compared to 49% of those households earning $30,000 or less.[90]

Resources on Wireless Access:

- Pew Internet and American Life Project: http://www.pewinternet.org
- The Digital Divide Network: http://www.digitaldividenetwork.org
- NYC Wireless: http://www.nycwireless.net
- Wireless Philadelphia Executive Committee: http://www.phila.gov/wireless/faqs.html

13 Home Ownership Plan For Workers

Submitted by Duane Fleming in Florida

One of the biggest problems for working people is how to afford a home and build a secure future. Another major problem is how to stabilize the housing and related industries, which drive 20% of the economy, and maintain employment to avoid devastating recessions.

The answer is the Home Ownership Plan (HOP), which is to be a tax-exempt savings account in the workplace for first-time home buyers. A key feature is the simple redirection of employee benefits. When young people enter the workplace, their employer can enroll them in the HOP, in lieu of enrolling them in a pension plan. The employer could then contribute to the HOP account the amount they would ordinarily pay into a pension plan.

In seven years, a person starting at $30,000 can save $50,000 toward a down payment. Couples can merge accounts with $50,000 to $100,000 to buy a home. They will have 25 years to save for retirement. The HOP more than pays for the tax exemptions from taxes generated by the housing and related industries.

Bio :: Duane Fleming

Duane Fleming, 69, works as economic program coordinator for the City of West Palm Beach, Florida. He's troubled by how hard it is for young people to save enough to make today's large down payments required to buy their first homes. "I look at fringe benefits and we've got health plans and 401(k) plans and pension plans—why not home ownership plans?" Fleming asks. A widower with one daughter, Heidi, Fleming felt so strongly about the idea that he convinced a member of Congress from Florida to introduce legislation to authorize it. "Unfortunately, the House committee only considered the cost of this program, but not the benefits that will flow from it," he says. Fleming has written a novel entitled The Trinity Constellation: Building a Third Way Globalization Path that he believes will advance the cause of workers everywhere.

Resources on Home Ownership:

- Center for Urban and Regional Policy:
  http://www.curp.neu.edu/aboutus.htm
- U.S. Department of Housing and Urban Development:
  http://www.hud.gov/offices/cpd/affordablehousing/index.cfm
- National Housing Trust Fund Campaign:
  http://www.nhtf.org/2006updatefeb.asp
- America's Neighbors: The Affordable Housing Crisis and the People it Affects. National Low Income Housing Coalition, February 2004.
- Urban Institute: http://www.urban.org/housing/index.cfm
- National Rural Housing Coalition: http://www.nrhcweb.org
- Laborers' International Union of North America: http://www.liuna.org

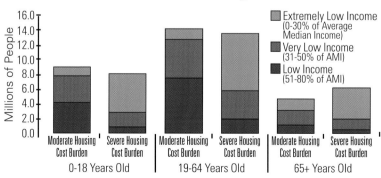

Number of Low-Income People With Moderate and Severe Housing Cost Burdens[91]

Facts :: Home Ownership

The heart of the American dream is home ownership, but too often that dream is out of reach. In 2004 the national median income was $43,318. That was only 61% of the $71,000 annual income needed to qualify to buy a $225,000 home.[92]

Median home prices rose by 26% from 2000 to 2005, but young adults' income went up less than 10%. Despite a cooling off of housing prices in early 2007, many young people now are spending 40% or more of their income on housing—substantially above the 30% that used to be the norm.[93]

About 40% of young people move back in with their parents after graduating from college—in part because they can't afford the escalating cost of housing. Many also face repayment of student loans as education aid has been cut by the Congress and the Administration.[94]

Under Fleming's Home Ownership Plan, the tax-exempt savings account for housing would result in some lost revenue for the government. But Fleming argues the plan would boost new home construction. With each new home generating tax revenue on average of about $25,000, he estimates the plan would more than pay for itself by generating an estimated $6.9 billion net gain to the U.S. Treasury each year.[95]

Union construction workers in the U.S. are about 17% more productive than workers at non-union projects, according to a three-year study by Independent Project Analysis. Experts cite high skill levels of union workers, demanding apprenticeship programs, and ongoing partnerships between construction unions and builders.[96]

Census data from 2005 shows that non-Hispanic whites have a 75% home ownership rate, while African-Americans have a 46% rate, Hispanics a 48% rate, and Asian-Americans a 59% rate.[97]

14 Do Not Tax Earnings For College Education

Submitted by John Collins in Massachusetts

Paying for college today has become a huge financial burden for most Americans. Students and/or their parents incur a great deal of debt to obtain a college degree. This extra debt hurts the productivity of the graduate and/or the parents for years. Many students must work while they go to school to help make ends meet, but this income doesn't go as far as it could because it is taxed.

My suggestion is that any full-time college student working to pay for school be exempt from income tax. And their parents should be allowed to take a deduction equal to the amount of their financial contribution—making both the students' and parents' earnings go further to pay for college expenses.

This could allow a student to afford to go to a better school or obtain a higher degree. A more educated and less debt-burdened workforce would help the overall outlook for the U.S. and our worldwide standing for generations to come.

Bio :: John Collins

John Collins, 46, runs his own small business as a manufacturing rep in western Massachusetts near the Berkshire mountains. With two sons in college, the cost of higher education is a huge issue for Collins. "My kids are a big inspiration to me and, like all parents, I want to see them get the best education possible," Collins says. His proposal would provide parents with a federal tax deduction equal to the amount they contribute to their children's college education. And full-time college students working to pay for their education would get an exemption from income tax on their pay. "I read about **Since Sliced Bread** in *Parade* magazine, cut out the article, left it on my desk where it got buried, and only found it weeks later," Collins says. "When I read it again, the idea came to me immediately." Collins graduated from University of Massachusetts-Amherst and earned an MBA from Western New England College. He trained his golden retriever "Strider" to be a therapy dog and volunteers at local nursing homes where the dog provides emotional support for residents. Collins also is a cyclist and stonecarves art objects.

Facts :: College Tuition Costs

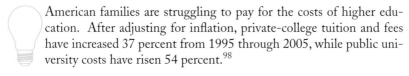

American families are struggling to pay for the costs of higher education. After adjusting for inflation, private-college tuition and fees have increased 37 percent from 1995 through 2005, while public university costs have risen 54 percent.[98]

You may be able to deduct qualified education expenses paid for yourself, spouse, or dependent. The tuition and fees deduction can reduce the amount of your income subject to tax by up to $4,000 and is taken as an adjustment to income.[99]

Two-thirds of college undergraduates graduate with debt. The U.S. Department of Education reports that among graduating seniors, the average debt load is approaching $20,000. That does not include any debt their parents might have incurred.[100]

In early 2006, Congress enacted proposals to pay for tax cuts for the wealthy in part by the biggest cuts in the history of student loan programs. The $12.7 billion reduction in student aid outraged both students and their parents. The changes include increases in loan rates under the Stafford program to 6.8 percent from 5.3 percent and in the PLUS loan program to 8.5 percent.[101]

Today, the average Pell Grant covers only 40 percent of college tuition, compared to 77 percent 25 years ago. The U.S. Department of Education has revised Pell Grant eligibility guidelines, effectively excluding almost 100,000 young people from the program and reducing grant money for another 1.2 million.[102]

Resources on College Costs/Student Aid:

- Tuition and Fees Deduction. Internal Revenue Service Publication #970, 2005: http://www.irs.gov/publications/p970/ch06.html
- Student Aid Action (PIRG): http://www.studentaidaction.com/aid.asp?id2=12611
- College Board: http://www.collegeboard.com/article/0,,6-29-0-4494,00.html
- Meeting College Costs: What You Need to Know Before Your Child and Your Money Leave Home. 2006 Edition: http://store.collegeboard.com/product_detail.asp?item=007212
- "What's the Cost of a College Education?" The Princeton Review: http://www.princetonreview.com/college/finance/articles/save/costcollege.asp
- "A Letter to Parents: We Are Drowning in Debt." By Elana Berkowitz and John Burton, Campus Progress: http://www.campusprogress.org/features/663/a-letter-to-parents-we-are-drowning-in-debt
- U.S. Student Association: http://www.usstudents.org
- American Association of Colleges and Universities: http://www.aacu-edu.org
- "The College Tax Breaks Explained." Smart Money: http://www.smartmoney.com/college/investing/index.cfm?story=education

15 Standardize Health Care Data

Submitted by Andrea Chen in California

It is estimated that "administrative costs" take over 30 cents of each U.S. health care dollar. This compares with under 20 cents for other nations. The difference is over $200 billion, 2% of GDP. Reducing these expenses is a goal.

I propose standardization of health care data and basic forms. A specific drug or procedure would have the same code among different providers and insurance companies. Basic patient information would also be in standard format. I would suggest new forms, such as lists of prescriptions and procedures—data which is often unorganized, and sometimes lost. Of course, providers could make exceptions. Consistency in naming can reduce costs in processing and passing information between organizations. It would also make billing more coherent.

Standardization of data structures makes it easier for computer programs to work together and for organizations to change programs. Like Internet protocols, they would provide a common language for a variety of approaches, increasing competition. Standards could also make it easier to gather data for research.

Bio :: Andrea Chen

Andrea Chen is a database programmer for the San Mateo-Foster City School District in northern California. Her proposal to standardize medical data evolved from experiences her husband had during frequent hospitalizations. "Often his data and test results weren't accessible," she says. "Hospital, doctors, insurers, business offices—they all use different ways of keeping records." Chen, 41, earned a degree in mathematics from Santa Clara University. She learned about **Since Sliced Bread** at smartmobs.com. Andrea's a Master Falconer who flies a Harris hawk in the East Bay area and San Joaquim Valley. She writes short stories and hopes to publish a novel. And she spends time working for anti-spam groups, tracing offenders and "trying to keep a lid on it."

Resources on Standardizing Health Data:

- "Personal Health Information: Data Comes Alive!" By Esther Dyson, September 2005. Release 1.0:
  http://www.release1-0.com/release1/abstracts.php?Counter=4886510
- Markle Foundation: http://www.markle.org
- "The Pros and Cons of Electronic Health Records." Consumer Reports, March 2006.
- American Health Quality Association: http://www.ahqa.org
- "Health Industry Under Pressure To Computerize." By Steve Lohr, *The New York Times*, Feb. 19, 2005.
- Patient Safety: Achieving a New Standard for Care. By Paul C. Tang, Institute of Medicine, 2004: http://www.iom.edu
- Service Employees International Union: http://www.seiu.org

REPORT: MEDICAL MISTAKES A LEADING CAUSE OF DEATH

Copyright © 1999 Star Tribune. Reprinted with permission.

Facts :: Standardizing Health Data

A national system of electronic medical records is being developed by the federal government, states, and health care providers. It would store and link the medical records of every American and electronically connect that data to providers, insurers, pharmacies, labs, and claims processors. The National Health Information Network could save thousands of lives and billions of dollars.[103]

The RAND Corporation estimates a potential savings in health care spending of $77 billion annually if 90% of the doctors and hospitals adopt an electronic medical records system. Savings would come from shorter hospital stays prompted by better-coordinated care and fewer duplicative tests and procedures.[104]

One concern about standardization of health care data and electronic medical records is patient privacy. As with credit reports, serious errors could creep into the system. With many different people entering data into your electronic health record, dangers exist that errors occur that could be life-threatening and that disclosures of certain potentially stigmatizing conditions could be harmful.[105]

The number of Americans spending more than a quarter of their income on medical costs climbed from 11.6 million in 2000 to 14.3 million in 2004. The annual cost of health insurance premiums for a typical family of four now exceeds $10,000.[106]

An electronic prescription system in Detroit filled more than 500,000 prescriptions in a year with more than 80,000 prescriptions changed or canceled due to drug-interaction alerts and 6,500 cases in which doctors learned of potentially allergic reactions.[107]

Kansas Medicaid launched a pilot program in 2006 to give physicians web-based access to patient information, including medications, allergies, immunizations, and clinic visits. Hospitals and clinics in Sedgwick County are participating, providing a community health record for 30,000 members of FirstGuard, a Medicaid HMO. In 2007, Kansas may expand the program statewide.[108]

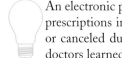

HEALTH CARE DATA

16 Teach Children Money Management

Submitted by Diana Nolen in Washington

Personal money management is a huge problem in America. Crushing credit card debt, overdue bills, and bankruptcies hang over our heads.

So many people just don't know how to handle money. They learn by trial-and-error during the time they should be building some wealth.

My suggestion is to put personal money management in the regular curriculum of all schools, starting with first grade and continuing through high school.

By the time a child reaches the teens, he/she should know all about compound interest, various investment plans, shopping wisely, and saving for the future.

Also, education would help them to resist the negative effects of being lured by advertisers to pointlessly spend money on "stuff," only to discard it when the commercials convince them they need some new "stuff." Give them the gift of financial freedom.

Bio :: Diana Nolen

Diana Nolen, 78, loves to write. She's completed two children's books—the first entitled "Money Doesn't Grow on Trees" and the second "Piggy Bank." Both aim to teach kids how to handle money and personal finances. Nolen's inspiration? "My #2 son is just horrible with money and he says 'But Mom, you were supposed to teach me'," she states. Lack of personal money management skills causes too many Americans to pile up debts they can't handle, so Nolen's idea is to start teaching money skills from first grade on. Nolen worked for the Small Tribes of Western Washington, a Native American group, and for construction companies. At age 68, she enrolled in Clover Park Technical College to study interior design and architectural drawing. Nolen entered 25 ideas in the contest, including a proposal that marijuana be legalized. "We're filling up our prisons with people on marijuana convictions and letting hardened criminals out," she says.

Resources on Money Management for Kids:

- Kids' Money: http://www.kidsmoney.org (Spanish available)
- Just Curious: Money Management:
  http://www.suffolk.lib.ny.us/youth/jcssmoney.html
- "Successfully Managing Money." National Association of Service and Conservation Corps: http://www.nascc.org/Successfully%20Managing%20Money%20-%20NEFE/index.html
- Family Education: Kids and Money: http://life.familyeducation.com/finances-and-money/allowance/34481.html
- "Teaching Kids About Money." By Mary Rowland: http://www.nea.org/money/pf030304.html
- Generation Debt. By Anya Kamenetz. Riverhead, 2006.
- Raising Money Smart Kids. By Janet Bodnar. Kaplan Education, 2005.
- "Young Money." InCharge Education Foundation: http://www.youngmoney.com
- Jump$tart Coalition for Personal Financial Literacy: http://www.jumpstart.org
- FirstGov for Kids
  http://www.kids.gov/k_money.htm
- Kids' Turn Central
  http://www.kidsturncentral.com/links/moneylinks.htm
- Ohio State University Family and Consumer Sciences
  http://credit.about.com/od/teachingourkids

Facts :: Money Management

The Federal Reserve Bank of New York offers financial literacy programs for elementary, middle, and high school students. They teach how to develop a monthly budget, how credit cards work and how to use them wisely, how to use the services of a bank, how the tax system works, and other issues.[109]

Lack of money management skills contributed to young adults ages 25 to 34 having the second-highest rate of bankruptcy in 2005 just after those 35 to 44. Credit-card debt held by consumers 18 to 34 soared 55% since 1992, to $4,088 on average.[110]

Federal legislation passed in 2002 authorizes $385 million for schools to develop practical money management courses for kindergarten through high school. But critics say the federal government has shortchanged funds to carry out the law.[111]

The Jump$tart Coalition, a financial literacy group, began to measure the financial literacy of high school seniors starting in 1995. Average scores stopped falling in 2004 and have begun to improve.[112]

American college students graduate with an average of nearly $20,000 in student loans. Even those with good financial skills face challenges finding jobs at a time of expanded outsourcing, increased use of contingent workers/temps, shrinking or non-existent health care benefits, high gas prices, and other problems.[113]

Consumers Union reported the bankruptcy law passed in Congress in 2005 does not contain a single restriction on reckless or predatory lending by creditors. Credit card companies have reaped substantial profits by targeting riskier borrowers, including young people who lack money-management skills.[114]

Dr. Benjamin Spock, in his best-selling book <u>Dr. Spock's Baby and Child Care</u>, urged that children be given allowances at age 6 or 7 to learn how to handle money. Spock said the allowance amount depends on family customs, finances, and the patterns of the community. Allowances should not be tied to chores, he said.[115]

Forbes magazine offers financial tips for college students including: use credit cards sparingly, pay credit card balances in full, get the best deal on a checking account, start saving, keep track of your spending, set a limit on entertainment, get a part-time job with tips, walk or ride a bike, look for student discounts, and don't eat out all the time.[116]

CAUTION
KEEP HANDS AND FEET
BETWEEN SIDE RAILS
DO NOT OVER-REACH

17 Pride of Skilled Working Hands

Submitted by Joey Diaz in California

How will America meet current and future needs for skilled craftspersons? How can we encourage thousands of young people not bound for college to consider a career in the trades as a professional, honorable way to gain valuable skills while earning a good living? I propose the creation of The Pride of Working Hands Program.

Purpose/Goals:
- Encourage thousands of boys and girls across the country at an early age to consider careers in one of many specialized skilled trades.
- Build early pride that using one's skilled hands in carrying out a skilled trade is a noble profession.
- Match students, schools, parents, trades' councils, construction associations, and home-improvement stores to training programs resulting in jobs. Some help would be provided free to low-income seniors while students finish their apprenticeships.

Participants:
- Elementary schools, career-day sponsors, parents, union trades councils, and thousands of home-improvement stores across the country that would provide training sites, materials, and also serve as resources for matching low-income seniors, community non-profits, etc. to students developing skills.

Bio :: Joey Diaz

Joey Diaz, 58, is a health consultant living in La Jolla, California. His idea for expanded programs for skilled trades training came after he saw an elderly widow have difficulty getting advice on buying a faucet from a young clerk at a home improvement store. With fewer opportunities for vocational education for non-college-bound youths, Diaz envisions expanded support for union apprenticeship and journeyman/woman programs. "I'm a handyman by nature and use it to relax," he says. Diaz has several patents, including one for small windmills for homes and RVs and another for a "human power flyer"—a personal aircraft that has had some "downside issues with liability insurance." Diaz grew up surfing before and after school and still goes out today, either on a longboard on calm days or his bubble nose when the surf's up. "The Beach Boys were the entertainment at my high school prom," he recalls. Fluent in Spanish and Portuguese, Diaz is married to a retired nurse and has a daughter now in college.

Resources on Skilled Hands:

- "Is A Career Or Technical Program Right for You?" The Princeton Review: http://www.princetonreview.com/cte/articles/plan/cteright.asp
- Vocational Information Center Trade and Technical Schools by Trade: http://www.khake.com/page68.html
- Center for Workforce Development: http://www.heldrich.rutgers.edu
- Culinary Training Academy UNITE-HERE Union: http://www.culinaryunion226.org
- State Directors of Vocational-Technical Education: http://wdcrobcolp01.ed.gov/Programs/EROD/org_list.cfm?category_ID=VTE
- Apprenticeship Training Resources: http://www.khake.com/page58.html

Earnings Advantage (in Percent) For Workers With College Degree Over High School Grads, 1975-2004[117]

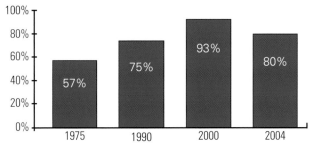

Facts :: Skilled Hands

There is a widening gap between the supply of skilled workers in America and the growing technical demands of the modern manufacturing workplace. A recent report states that more than 80% of 815 manufacturing companies surveyed are experiencing an overall shortage of qualified workers, such as machinists, craft workers, and technicians.[118]

The 2005 Skills Gap Report issued by the National Association of Manufacturers urged employers to invest at least 3% of payroll in training for their workforces. Despite that recommendation, the NAM survey reported that 75% of its companies fail to spend that much on skill-building.[119]

With heightened global competition and corporate cost-cutting, more companies want highly skilled workers, but don't want to pay to hone their skills. Yet more and more jobs involve fairly sophisticated technologies that require highly skilled workers. The dilemma: corporations complain about a skills gap and the shortage of skilled workers, yet those same firms have reduced or eliminated funding for employee training.[120]

Vocational education has waned as the public has come to believe that almost all high school graduates should go to college. College-educated workers have a significant earnings advantage over high school graduates—the so-called "college premium." But from 2000 to 2004, college grads have suffered a 5.2% fall in real earnings while high school graduates have seen real earnings increase by 1.6%.[121]

Starting around 1970, non-union construction firms expanded by undercutting union contractors. They pushed down wages, driving experienced workers from the industry, but seldom contributed to apprentice training programs. Today, the industry is starved for skilled workers. What homeowners and other construction customers have gained from cheaper labor, they lost in lower productivity and shoddy quality.[122]

One of the most successful skilled hands programs is the Culinary Training Academy (CTA) in Las Vegas run by the UNITE-HERE Local Union 226. When you apply for employment at a Vegas hotel, you go to the union hall for a skills assessment. If you need or want training, you go to the CTA—funded entirely by employers with a curriculum developed jointly by management and labor. More than 20,000 have graduated from the Academy and 75% are still employed by Vegas hotels.[123]

SKILLED HANDS

18 Mortgages for Abandoned Houses

Submitted by Melanie Jones in Indiana

Problem: Dilapidated houses, ruined often from landlords and tenants not doing upkeep (they don't live there or they don't own the house, so they don't care), are abandoned. They continue to deteriorate, look awful, and attract rats and crime. It costs cities $5,000 to demolish such houses.

Solution: Federal or State Low-Interest Mortgage Program.
- No interest accrues during the first five years of a loan if the buyer remains in good standing.
- House must cost 50% or less of market value for a similar house in good condition.
- Buyers must make 200% or less of poverty level income, agree to live in the house for five years, and must previously have been renting.
- Buyer can escrow additional loan money to use for house repairs, up to a $50,000 total mortgage amount, and must use receipts to prove escrow money goes toward repairs.
- Buyer must live in the house within six months after closing. Mortgage payments don't begin until residency.

Benefits:
- Brings more income into impoverished areas.
- Cleaner and safer neighborhoods.
- No money paid to demolish houses.
- Makes homeownership possible for low-income families.

Bio :: Melanie Jones

Many large, beautiful houses that lined the streets of Anderson, Indiana back when the auto industry was booming now have fallen into disrepair. Melanie Jones, a grad student in theology at Anderson University, wants to see those crumbling homes restored to house low-income families. Her proposal argues for a mortgage program providing low-interest mortgage loans to "rehab" dilapidated houses that often are abandoned. "I'm passionate about urban issues and really believe we need to support sustainable development," Jones says. She bought one of those houses for less than $25,000 and has spent hundreds of hours fixing it up. Jones lives there with her dog Bichinha (Portuguese for "little beast"), a cat, and a hamster. She plays clarinet and saxophone and loves politics. "I've got a 'Wesley Clark '08' bumper sticker on my '91 Park Avenue," she says.

Vista Rotary Club

Resources on Reclaiming Housing:

- ACORN (Association of Community Organizations for Reform Now): http://www.acorn.org
- Department of Housing and Urban Development: http://www.hud.gov/offices/hsg/sfh/203k/203k--df.cfm
- National Low Income Housing Coalition: http://www.nlihc.org
- Center for Community Change Housing Trust Fund Project: http://www.communitychange.org/issues/housingtrustfunds/ whatarehousingtf/
- The Crisis in America's Housing. Edited by Lisa Ranghelli. January 2005 http://www.nlihc.org/research/index.htm
- Habitat for Humanity: http://www.habitat.org
- Housing America: http://www.housingamerica.net

Facts :: Reclaiming Housing

Atlanta, Cleveland, Detroit, and other cities have moved to streamline the process of monitoring and reselling derelict properties. Cleveland pioneered in the '90s when unpaid property taxes on abandoned structures in Cuyahoga County surged toward $100 million. Cleveland and later Atlanta created "land-bank authorities" that can waive or forgive delinquent property taxes. The land banks take foreclosed property that didn't sell at auctions where the minimum sales price can't be less than the taxes owed. The land banks work closely with non-profits to expand low- and moderate-income housing.[124]

A 2005 study by ACORN showed that minorities often must pay significantly higher loan rates as they attempt to buy or rehab their homes. Nationally, African-Americans were 2.7 times more likely than whites to receive a high-cost loan when refinancing. Latinos were 1.4 times more likely to have to pay for high-cost financing.[125]

Genesee County, Michigan launched a Land Reutilization Fund that helps rehabilitate abandoned houses. Its largest city, Flint, had more than 12% of its housing stock empty after losing 60,000 high-wage jobs related to the auto industry. The Fund took in more than $4 million during its first three years. It can be used to help property owners facing severe hardship keep their properties.[126]

Detroit has 12,000 abandoned homes—a byproduct of decades of lay-offs at the city's auto plants and white flight to the suburbs. As residents and businesses have relocated, about 36 square miles of vacant land have been left behind—roughly the size of San Francisco and about a quarter of Detroit's total landmass. The city tears down about 1,500 to 2,000 abandoned houses each year, but that's about the same number being left behind, so the backlog stays roughly the same.[127]

Freddie Mac committed $5 million to purchase mortgages from Key Bank and Trust to see that scores of empty foreclosed houses in Baltimore can be rehabilitated. The initiative is a collaboration with the City and County of Baltimore, the St. Ambrose Housing Aid Center and the Govans Economic Management Senate (GEMS). More than 100 houses were scheduled to be renovated.[128]

The federal Department of Housing and Urban Development (HUD) offers a rehabilitation mortgage insurance program known as "203(k)." It enables homebuyers to finance both the purchase and the cost of rehabilitation through a single mortgage. The program deals with the common problem that potential buyers of dilapidated housing first must get financing to purchase the property, then obtain additional financing to fix up the house, and then find a permanent mortgage after the work is done to pay off the interim loans.[129]

ABANDONED HOUSES

19 Access to Capital For Small Businesses

Submitted by Susan Almeida in Florida

Issue: Maintaining U.S. household income in the face of across-the-board global competition for income-producing vocations. Climbing the value chain ultimately fails—India and China can train more of any profession, including engineers, marketers, CEOs—based on sheer population. We are not leveraging America's strongest competitive advantage: efficient capital markets and entrepreneurship, which are stubbornly difficult for other countries to duplicate. U.S. small and medium businesses (SMBs) provide 90% of jobs, yet have no efficient capitalization mechanism. So 90% of SMB failures are from lack of capital. SMBs are not efficiently serviced by stock exchanges, venture/angel funding, or local banks.

Solution: Create an agency—"ProdiMae/ServiMac"—similar to FannieMae/FreddieMac's missions, but for SMBs. It would provide an efficient secondary market for equity/debt so SMBs can get funding through local funders who would then sell those instruments in the secondary market—unleashing national sources of capital for SMBs.

Benefits: Tremendous opportunities would open up for working men and women to become thriving business owners/employers or well-paid employees of those companies.

Bio :: Susan Almeida

Susan Almeida, 47, runs a real estate practice in southwest Florida specializing in waterfront properties. She spent 20 years as an executive in the high-tech sector after earning a degree in electrical engineering from Worcester Polytechnic Institute in Massachusetts. Almeida saw how venture capital and "angel" investors gave firms the funding to turn ideas into profitable companies. "But many small businesses fail in the first five years due to a lack of capital, not because of bad business plans," she says. Her winning contest idea addresses that by creating secondary markets for equity and debt so small- and medium-sized businesses can raise capital through local funders. She likes hiking, biking, boating, and fishing and enjoys her red toy poodle named "Annie" and her Yorkie named "Lucy."

Facts :: Small Business and Capital

 More than half of small businesses fail in the first year and 95% fail within the first five years, according to the U.S. Small Business Administration (SBA). A leading cause of small business failure is insufficient capital (money).[130]

Experts say someone starting a new business should have access to a sum of money (capital) at least equal to the projected revenue for the first year of business in addition to expenses. For example, if an entrepreneur thinks she will generate $100,000 in revenues in the first year with $150,000 in start-up expenses, then she should have no less than $250,000 available.[131]

 Existing sources of start-up capital include the owner using personal assets; partnering with someone with capital; funding from a "venture capitalist;" Small Business Administration loan guarantees; bank loans or lines of credit; and financing using credit card debt (usually a bad idea).[132]

Fannie Mae is a private company established by the federal government to expand the flow of home mortgage money by creating a secondary market, similar to what might be done under Almeida's plan. Fannie Mae does not loan money directly to home buyers, but purchases home mortgages from the initial lenders such as banks. The company issues securities in exchange for pools of mortgages from lenders and essentially helps ensure sufficient capital for lenders to make home loans to individuals.[133]

 Small business often is portrayed as not only the most powerful engine of economic growth, but also as an agent of innovation, cost reduction, and flexibility. This favorable image—accurate or not—has given small business a considerable influence on public policy.[134]

Resources on Small Business and Capital:

- Fannie Mae: http://www.fanniemae.com
- U.S. Small Business Administration: http://www.sba.gov
- Economic Policy Institute: http://www.epi.org
- How To Raise Capital: Techniques and Strategies for Financing and Valuing Your Small Business. By Jeffrey Timmons, Stephen Spinelli, and Andrew Zacharakis, McGraw-Hill, 2004.
- Center for Economic and Policy Research: http://www.cepr.net

20 National Service Scholarship Program

Submitted by Adam Lyons in Rhode Island

Problems: 1. Rising cost of college education for parents and students. 2. Pending shortages in government workforce due to pending retirement of large numbers of baby-boomers. 3. Deterioration of civic understanding and involvement at the local, state, and national level. 4. General workforce knowledge gap of government-industry capabilities and opportunities.

Solution: Use the Armed Services' highly successful Reserve Officer Training Corps scholarships as a model for a larger government-wide education and workforce program. Offer two- and four-year scholarship opportunities with service obligations post-graduation.

Benefits: 1. Would free up some of the economic burden of education costs that could then be redirected to retirement, savings, health care, etc. 2. Provide a systematic influx of young people with the energy and innovative ideas that are desperately needed within the government to affect change necessary in the 21st century. 3. Those who leave government service after their obligation will provide the catalyst to reinvigorate the sense of service and community at all levels, and have knowledge of government enabling them to capitalize on capabilities and opportunities along the government-industry seam.

Bio :: Adam Lyons

Adam Lyons, a Lieutenant Commander in the U.S. Navy, works in Bremerton, Washington for Carrier Strike Group 3. He received an email sent to Naval voting assistance officers encouraging military personnel to submit ideas to the **Since Slice Bread** competition. "I thought the contest was neat and I forwarded the email to some friends and family," says Lyons, who is 34. A 1994 graduate of the U.S. Naval Academy, he earned master's degrees from University of Maryland and the Naval War College. Lyons' proposal for a National Service Scholarship evolved from his view that the Defense Department's ROTC program works well in recruiting young people in return for money for college. "We need to attract the brightest minds into government service by offering to help reduce the high cost of college education," Lyons said. His wife is an elementary education teacher who's currently a full-time mother caring for their two young children. Lyons enjoys hiking, martial arts, and reading history—particularly the American colonial/founding period.

Resources on National Service:

- Corporation for National and Community Service:
  http://www.nationalservice.gov
- Partnership for Public Service: http://www.ourpublicservice.org
- ROTC FAQs:
  http://www.collegeboard.com/article/0,,4-24-0-36978,00.html
- American Federation of Government Employees: http://www.afge.org
- AmeriCorps: http://www.americorps.gov
- Online Publications on National Service:
  http://www.nationalserviceresources.org/resources/online_pubs/index.php
- Seasons of Service, Points of Light Foundation:
  http://www.pointsoflight.org/programs/seasons

WHAT'S NEXT FOR SINCE SLICED BREAD?

SinceSlicedBread.com

Facts :: National Service Scholarships

 The Reserve Officer Training Corps (ROTC) provides scholarships to finance college followed by a mandatory period of service in the military. Most cadets incur a four-year active-duty commitment in the Army, Navy, or Air Force. Scholarship amounts vary, but can go up to $20,000 accrued.[135]

One of the best national service programs, the National Civilian Community Corps (NCCC), has involved more than 11,000 18- to 24-year-olds in service programs, including recovery work in areas hit by Hurricane Katrina. The program, which President Bush embraced as part of his "compassionate conservatism" in 2001, has completed 6,249 projects including rebuilding 5,500 houses, tutoring 319,000 students and building 7,800 miles of hiking trails. The Administration decided in early 2006 to shut down the program.[136]

 Speaking at a Princeton forum on recruiting students to public service, then-Senator Paul Sarbanes (D-MD) noted that "a small truth that government can't do everything has transformed into a big falsehood that government can't do anything." To encourage young people to enter government service, Princeton announced a "Scholars in the Nation's Service" fellowship program.[137]

A national service scholarship program aimed at exposing young people to public sector work could help deal with the growing problem of federal brain drain. About 44% of all federal workers become eligible to retire over the next five years and 61% reach retirement eligibility four years later.[138]

 The need for a new influx of bright young people choosing careers in government service is underscored by the turnover to come. About 40% of the Dept. of Homeland Security managers can retire by 2009; 42% of the Senior Executive Service by 2010; and 94% of the Social Security administrative law judges by 2010.[139]

During the 2004 presidential campaign, Senator John Kerry urged a "Service for College" initiative through which Americans could give two years of national service and earn the equivalent of their state's four-year public college tuition in exchange.[140]

 According to a 2006 civic-engagement briefing by the Corporation for National and Community Service, 38% of students between the ages of 12 and 18 participate in school-based service. Of this group, 77% experience "quality" service-learning, including writing or reflecting on the experience in class, participating in planning the activity, or participating in regular community service for one semester.[141]

SERVICE SCHOLARSHIPS

21 Shift From Job-Based Health Insurance

Submitted by Bridget "Brydie" Ragan in Washington

Job-based health care insurance is very bad for our economy for two main reasons. First, job-based health care drives up the cost of American products because corporations have to pay costly health care premiums, making it very difficult for us to compete globally. Other countries have national health care insurance, so their product costs are lower.

Secondly, job-based health insurance restricts the innovative spirit of the American people. Our workers stay in jobs they don't like, rather than making career changes or starting their own businesses, because they are afraid to live without health insurance.

We need national health insurance, and I propose that we fund the program with a special sales tax so that EVERYONE pays into the system at least a little bit.

If we have national health care insurance, the cost of American products would go down and large companies could expand into global markets. We could keep jobs at home.

Also, our workers would have job mobility, which would make our existing companies better, and would create a safety net for new entrepreneurs.

Bio :: Bridget Ragan

Nobody calls her Bridget. "Brydie" Ragan, 52, has been a part-time tutor in writing and English as a second language. Her interest in universal health care that's not linked to employment came after she became ill in 1997 while attempting to start her own business. "I was under-insured, got sick, and ended up declaring personal bankruptcy," she recalls. During her years in the high-tech sector, Ragan saw co-workers trapped in jobs they would have quit were it not for the good health insurance provided through their employers. "Every other industrialized country in the world has universal health care," Ragan says. "We should have it here and it shouldn't be tied to employment." She recently developed a health care presentation she'll be emphasizing in a new professional speaking business. Brydie is married and has two stepchildren. She enjoys abstract painting.

Resources on Health Care and Employment:

- Americans for Health Care: http://www.americansforhealthcare.org
- "Future of Employer-Based Health Benefits." Bureau of National Affairs Web Watch: http://www.bna.com/webwatch/futurehealth.htm
- "Fair Share Health Care Sweeping the Nation": http://www.seiu.org/action_center/jan_fair_share.cfm
- "On the Fringe: The Substandard Benefits of Workers in Part-Time, Temporary, and Contract Jobs." The Commonwealth Fund, 2005.
- "The Employer-Based Health Care System Is In Crisis." Labor Research Association, June 6, 2004: http://www.laborresearch.org/story2.php/357
- Health Insurance/Costs: Employer-Sponsored Insurance. Kaiser Family Foundation: http://www.kff.org/insurance/employer.cfm

Rates of Middle-Income Adults Who Are Uninsured Or Receiving Employment-Based Health Insurance[142]

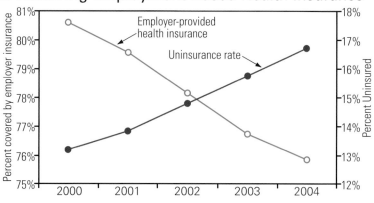

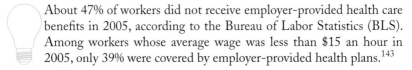

Facts :: Health Care and Employment

About 47% of workers did not receive employer-provided health care benefits in 2005, according to the Bureau of Labor Statistics (BLS). Among workers whose average wage was less than $15 an hour in 2005, only 39% were covered by employer-provided health plans.[143]

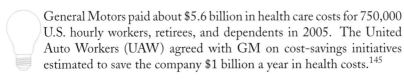

About a third of the nearly $2 trillion in annual health care spending in the United States goes to clerical matters, not treatment, according to researchers at Harvard University. This is due primarily to the wide array of private insurers involved. Experts say a single-payer health care system, similar to Medicare, could provide universal coverage for all Americans at a long-term cost to taxpayers well below what's now paid annually by employers and workers.[144]

General Motors paid about $5.6 billion in health care costs for 750,000 U.S. hourly workers, retirees, and dependents in 2005. The United Auto Workers (UAW) agreed with GM on cost-savings initiatives estimated to save the company $1 billion a year in health costs.[145]

U.S. workers' contributions and out-of-pocket health care expenses in 2006 were estimated to rise 11.6%, while wages were estimated to increase 3.6%. For a person making $40,000 per year, that increase in health-care costs would take about 23% of their overall salary gains.[146]

The U.S. repeatedly loses jobs to other countries that have government-provided health care systems. Toyota, for example, chose in early 2006 to build a 1,300-worker factory in Canada where workers are $4-5 an hour cheaper to employ due in part to the taxpayer-funded health-care system in Canada.[147]

Nearly 38% of all workers are employed in smaller businesses where less than two-thirds of firms now offer health benefits. Some 266,000 companies dropped their health coverage between 2000 and 2005. About 90% of those firms have fewer than 25 employees.[148]

About 58% of uninsured adults report having changed or lost jobs in 2003. "Job lock" keeps others in positions they might have left, if not for fear of losing health coverage. Job mobility of husbands is 25% to 32% lower when their wives do not have employment-based health insurance.[149]

The number of uninsured has increased by six million since the year 2000. Companies that do offer health insurance often require workers to contribute a larger share toward their coverage. As a result, an increasing number of Americans have opted not to take advantage of job-based health insurance because they cannot afford it.[150]

More Contest Ideas

More than 22,000 ideas were submitted during the **Since Sliced Bread** contest. In addition to the 21 contest winners in this book, the following submissions were among many that stirred comment and reaction at the SinceSlicedBread.com website.

Tie Minimum Wage To Congressional Pay
Submitted by Jan Chism W. in Nebraska

The minimum wage needs to be raised and increases tied to the increases in Congressional pay.

Reduce Size Of Military; Invest At Home
Submitted by Jack E. in Mississippi

The issue is the inability of the United States to responsibly fund social programs and simultaneously maintain an immense military machine and civil service apparatus. Globalization drains jobs with good health and retirement benefits, replacing them with part-time, no-benefit Wal-Mart type jobs. There is no stopping the march of globalization; to think otherwise is to dream.

It is time to drastically reduce the size of our military/industrial complex and our overseas commitments and alliances. We should redirect the money into some much-needed domestic construction projects. Modernization of our railway system and creation of a network of good intermediate-distance high-speed passenger rail service would produce good jobs and prepare us better for the coming energy supply crunches. Spending money on a decent universal health care system would protect the ever-increasing number of us who cannot afford medical services.

To abandon the illusion of "superpower" is also to abandon the hatred generated by what is widely perceived as U.S. imperialism. This step will improve national anti-terror security more than 50,000 civil servants ever could.

Favor Currency You Redeem As Tax Credit
Submitted by Scott C. in New Jersey

This contest is for out-of-the-box thinking so here's a strange solution, but it has merit.

I wanted to come up with a solution that would increase community involvement on a local level to help make the community a better place.

My solution is to create a line of non-spendable "favor currency" initially distributed by city-run organizations; however, once in circulation, it can be given to anyone helping anyone else in the community.

Let's say you volunteer to help at a food shelter, community event, or work as a volunteer teacher, fire fighter, etc. They get x amount of favor currency from that organization. Then if you help that person do something, they can pass the favor currency on to you. This way the currency gets distributed among folks that help others.

Photos by Earl Dotter.

At the end of the year, favor currency is redeemable as a tax credit. The redeemed favor currency is then re-circulated back to the city-run organizations.

The goal is to reward good folks for doing good things around the community.

Legalize It!
Submitted by Stephen W. in Alabama

Currently, our courts and penal system are clogged with marijuana offenders. Legalizing marijuana would free thousands of non-violent 'criminals,' giving families back their fathers, mothers, sons, and daughters. Legalization would also save different levels of government millions, if not billions, of dollars in failing law enforcement efforts. It would also allow medical users in all states to get medication they need legally and without fear. Besides lowering government costs associated with funding inmates and the endless trials that accompany them, entire new industries would be opened up to family farmers—a struggling group in America. Industrial hemp would become a staple for paper, plastics, food, biofuel, and other commodities as it is a renewable resource. Farming of hemp and marijuana would require new companies to be created to innovate new farming technologies for this now-banned plant, as well as companies to be created to manufacture, distribute, and sell these two different but related plants. Legalizing marijuana would also eliminate a huge section of the black market, effectively putting a stop to organized crime.

Itemized Tax Receipts
Submitted by Raphael M. in New York

There is a simple way to ensure that more voters monitor how their taxes are spent. The U.S. Treasury should provide every taxpayer with an itemized receipt of how their tax dollars were spent. People should not have to go online and research to find out precisely how the government spent their tax

dollars. A bipartisan committee should calculate what percentage of government spending goes to each government program as well as choose a non-politically biased description of each program. The percentages and descriptions should then be calculated and mailed to every taxpayer.

It's one thing to know in the abstract how the government spends its money. It is another to receive an exact description of how much of your hard-earned cash went to the military, how much to farm subsidies, how much to foreign aid, etc. A financially informed electorate is more likely to be active in ensuring government spending is prudent and responsible.

"WHO Am I Voting For?" Pamphlet
Submitted by Elizabeth D. in New York

A questionnaire should be developed specific to each elected position, for every candidate to fill out. This questionnaire will be the basis for the development of a 2-page "Voting Information Pamphlet" made widely available to all voters a month before elections—through the mail, at libraries, on the Internet, etc.

The information will be provided in a clear and concise manner and will cover the following areas:

1. Mini-resume—career and academic history; professional organizations; professional and public projects;
2. Endorsements—individuals and organizations;
3. Voting history of previous term on hot topics—decided in questionnaire development process (incumbent);

4. Positions on hot topics—mini-paragraph from candidate on each;
5. Promised public plans/projects;
6. Initiated/completed public plans/projects/bills;
7. List of interviews and writings on hot topics—where to get them from websites/publications/recordings;
8. Personal statement;
9. Contact information;
10. Candidate's website.

All pamphlets will be standardized for each election so that every candidate is objectively and fairly represented.

One Subject Per Law
Submitted by Judith G. in Missouri

No legislature can pass a bill that contains more than one subject.

No amendments to any bill that do not directly pertain to the main subject are allowed. No riders are allowed, period.

Pork-barrel projects, raises in salary for elected officials, funding for research that doesn't need to be done, and other such things that currently get attached to serious bills would be by themselves and, therefore, very difficult to justify.

Our law code would be simpler: it could be organized by subject. Precedents would be easier to find, and the average person would have a chance to understand the written law.

Our representatives in Congress would be more accountable to their constituents: the public could see who voted for wasteful projects and could turn them out the next election cycle.

Our economy would benefit: politicians wouldn't be spending our money on useless, wasteful activities—and Congress might just succeed at living within its means, as 20-year-old Public Law 95-435 says it will.

Consumer Credit And Debt
Submitted by anonymous in Washington

The Issue: Consumer credit.

The Problem:
People living beyond their means.
Consumer debt has sky-rocketed.
Savings are down.

Possible Solutions:
Consumer credit legislation that would do the following:

- All credit cards would have a membership fee and a yearly fee. This would discourage people from having too many credit cards.
- Make it illegal for credit card companies to up credit limits; instead make it a requirement that people apply for credit increases, and make them prove their ability to pay.
- Except in times of emergency, make all credit purchases have a time limit, thus making people pay off existing debt before incurring more.
- Except for debt consolidation, do not allow credit transfers from one credit card company to another.
- Make FICO (credit) scores be determined by actual ability to pay, rather than by debt-to-limit leveraging.

The Benefit: More accountability by both the lender and the consumer; consumers living within their means making for a healthier economy and a reduction in consumer stress.

Make Election Day a National Holiday
Submitted by Sarah B. in Pennsylvania

Working people are less likely to vote than are the affluent. Understandably, workers have busy lives and inflexible work schedules. As such, they are effectively excluded from the democratic process. We need to make Election Day a national holiday to ensure that everyone truly has the opportunity to participate in our democracy.

Increasing voter turnout will make our democracy more genuine, and allow working people to have their concerns addressed at the local, state, and national levels. This is a wide-reaching reform that will have broader impact than any given economic or social policy. It will allow people to actually participate in forming the policies (or at least, electing the politicians who form the policies) that affect their lives in innumerable ways.

Anyone who believes that democracy is a good idea must think that increasing voter turnout is a good idea. It's hard to argue with ensuring access to the ballot box. I suspect that any politicians or organizations backing this idea would enjoy significant public support.

Help Workers Combat Outsourcing
Submitted by anonymous in New York

Outsourcing is a fact of life. We need a strategy. At issue is how best to protect American workers from the threat of downsizing due to massive outsourcing of jobs to foreign markets. The answer is not to impose economic barriers to outsourcing that place the U.S. at a competitive disadvantage relative to other nations.

First, we should promote unionization, collective bargaining, higher minimum wages, and health and job safety standards in developing countries. Over the long term, this would raise the cost of foreign labor—reducing its competitive advantage. Tie these reforms to government loans and financial aid.

Second, form a council of economists, job-trend experts, and governors to assess (a) which careers face more risk of being outsourced in the next 10 years; (b) where we should fight to maintain our edge in innovation; and (c) where we should capitulate to overwhelming market forces. Offer scholarships, grants, training and skill sets for careers and fields where we are more likely to have a sustained competitive advantage that will be more viable in the global economy.

City Planning vs. Traffic Congestion
Submitted by anonymous in Washington

The Issue: City planning and traffic congestion.

The Problem: Traffic congestion wastes time, money, and energy and causes air, water, and noise pollution.

The Solution: Divert a portion of gas taxes for new concepts in traffic planning and implementation.

Suggestions: In residential areas that are laid out in grids (the vast majority), change them to one-way streets, taking one lane and making a bike and golf cart path out of it, and leave one lane for regular cars. Eventually, tie these grids into secondary arterials that have the same configuration, to move people freely about the city, or tie them into park-and-ride stops for mass transit.

Build shopping centers/strip malls with buildings close together and parking garages on the outer perimeter. Require efficient, non-polluting transport to and from parking. Also, make people-moving covered walkways, and bike and golf cart lanes available.

The Benefit: Stimulate the economy, reduce pollution, reduce wasted time, money, and energy.

Close Wage Gap, Stimulate Economy
Submitted by Jeffrey M. in Texas

Close the wage gap between workers and corporate executives.

Set a point between CEO and average hourly worker pay, for example 1/50th. Implement a tax on the corporation based on all money paid per employee over that ratio. Conversely, have a tax break for all worker pay under that ratio. Since execs would be loath to cut their own pay, they would need to raise worker pay. Also have a de facto excess profit tax in the form of a law requiring that an amount relative to any increase in share price or dividend paid be added to the hourly wage of workers for that quarter.

This would raise the standard of living of average Americans back to where it should be. A middle class with disposable income could raise the nation's savings rate to where it should be. They could buy homes, creating construction jobs. They could buy durable goods, increasing factory orders and creating more jobs, etc. This would increase profits, thus pay and continue the whole upward trend.

Funding For Health Care
Submitted by anonymous in Ohio

Americans are drowning in debt to credit card companies. The federal government could create a national credit card that could be issued to all credit-worthy Americans. They could charge an interest rate that is slightly lower than competing major credit cards (i.e. Visa, MasterCard, American Express) from financial institutions, yet high enough to generate sufficient revenues to fund health care for the most needy in our society. Instead of interest payments going to wealthy banks, the interest would instead be "invested" in the welfare of the American people.

We Need Good Public Transportation
Submitted by Paul B. in New Mexico

It is only the shabby condition of our public transport system that makes people reluctant to use it. Public transport is heavily used in cities where it is quick and reliable throughout. Rather than loopy routes and irregular schedules, there should be a grid. Buses should run up and down all major streets, maybe smaller buses for smaller streets. You should be able to board any bus for an hour after paying.

Not having to maintain a car makes it more feasible for people to take lower-paying jobs. Like a passive pay raise, the absence of a car makes it more feasible for people to take lower-paying jobs. Like a passive pay raise, the absence of car-related costs (maintenance, insurance, loan payment) puts money in the pocket of the worker. Plus, public transport is more reliable than a marginal automobile, thus reducing lateness and absence due to accidents, traffic, or breakdowns. Businesses spend less money providing parking space for employees.

Expanding public transport creates jobs for drivers and mechanics and might pay for itself in reduced road maintenance alone.

Election Channel.org
Submitted by Christopher C. in Hawaii

The problem is the influence of big money on government and politicians.

My idea is the Election Channel and Election.org. Every office for election from dog catcher to the President would only be allowed at these locations. A structured format of debates, biographies, position statements, etc. would be required of all candidates. It could be limited to six to nine months before an election, run and repeated 24/7, and regionalized on cable and the Internet.

The channels and website used would be owned by the people and facilities made available for the media production candidates would need. All political advertising would be banned. The Election Channel and Election. org could have non-political commercials to help pay for costs. This would not prevent candidates from talking at public events and gatherings and film of that can be used at Election Channel.org.

This would help by making government more responsive to average Americans and their needs because more average Americans would be able to run for office with the outrageous money barrier removed.

Democracy/Economy Rely On Education
Submitted by Elizabeth E. in Arizona

The Issue:
Our educational system fails many who cannot reach their potential.

The Plan:
Open schools to all needing an education. Provide free education for everyone. Open schools year-round, evenings, and weekends for workers. Primary role of prisons=education/rehabilitation centers.

The Funding:
Fund education as though our future depends on it—it does. Property taxes are obsolete/unfair—use income/sales/VAT. Corporations/businesses pay education taxes—they benefit directly. Make 529 accounts "family education accounts." Direct unneeded prison $ to education.

The Teachers:

Attract qualified/inspired teachers, pay salaries consistent with degrees to compete with industry for the best minds. Make public teacher salaries tax-free. Employ experts as part-time adjunct teachers. Create elder-teaching corps to mentor/tutor.

The Curriculum:

Focus on interests, not subjects; skills, not tests. Students advance at individual pace in multi-age settings. Flexible options for college, trade schools, work-study, work time, national service. Relate societal roles, jobs, real world to education.

The Benefits:

Expanded education sector creates jobs. Closing the compensation gap between highest and lowest incomes will add nearly $250 billion to GDP and $80 billion in tax revenue. Quality of life and satisfaction would improve for all Americans.

"Sliced Bread"; A Catalyst For Hope
Submitted by anonymous in Washington

Build cities for the future.

The United States has a huge landmass and yet the majority (80+%) live in urban areas, while small-town America is drying up. Why? The answer is simple; people migrate to where the economic opportunity is, and for the last 100 years that has been to urban areas.

Using "Sliced Bread" as a catalyst, let's put our ideas together with regional planners, economic developers, labor unions, environmentalists, public safety officials, parks and recreation, health care and education activists to plan new cities, or rebuild those that have been devastated by natural disasters.

Let's start with the many good ideas generated in this contest; pick an area that needs to (re)establish economic stability, convene a task force funded by government, industry, environmental, and labor groups and begin the process of building cities for the future.

Let us actually bring together the people who have entered this contest and find a way for them to move forward, in co-operation, to build a better America.

If we build it, they will come!!

Have Computers Do Redistricting
Submitted by anonymous in California

Our democracy is broken when who gets to decide the boundaries of a political district is more important than how voters vote, and that's the way it works today.

Government officials don't care what voters think anymore, because they know their election districts have been drawn in a way that keeps them in office. It doesn't matter if people come up with ideas to solve the problems of ordinary Americans as long as politicians don't need to care what ordinary Americans think.

That's why districts should be drawn by a simple computer formula that politicians can't manipulate. For example, the rule could be: "Of all the possible ways to draw districts, find a way that makes sure each district is within 0.1% population of the other districts, and which has the smallest total weighted average distance to the population center of each district."

The exact rule doesn't matter as long as it is completely objective and politicians can't manipulate it. Districts should be determined by where people live, not by what job politicians want to have.

A National Enviro-Economic Model
Submitted by Gary K. in Washington

Economic indicators are up—and so is hunger. Working Americans face pay cuts and disappearing jobs and pensions. There are threats to the economy: looming shortages of oil and water; global warming; overpopulation; runaway deficits; ballooning public and private debt; and unsustainable costs for Social Security and health care.

There's no shortage of solutions. The challenge is to identify the good ideas AND convince decision-makers to act. Existing economic models can help by predicting outcomes, but they're limited and unreliable: consider the diverse predictions for NAFTA (North American Free Trade Agreement).

Hence my proposal: Launch a national effort to understand and model the U.S. economy, an economic Apollo Project. Bring together top economists, mathematicians, computer scientists, software engineers, and graphics experts. Build and apply an evolving national economic model with environmental and social dimensions. Develop in parallel:

- Net-based data input tools;
- A Net-accessible database;
- Simulation tools; and
- Animated graphic outputs.

We have technologies for modeling complex systems, from weather to airplanes. Let's use them to design a crash-proof, worker-friendly economy.

Building A Skills Army For America

Submitted by Dennis B. in Michigan

In a disaster, how do you move a million people and fix everything? You build a "skills army." Pressed into service, volunteers start doing new work. It dawns on volunteers that working in a skilled trade may not be such a bad idea in our competitive economy. The idea is to connect existing organizational efforts to deal with disasters (National Guard, Red Cross, FEMA, utilities, etc.) with organizations that provide skilled jobs training (trade schools, community colleges, military, etc.) to not only rebuild a stricken area, but also to provide a new workforce for the larger economy. A President/Congress/Military/Business "brains-trust" can figure out a way to realign many existing agencies to achieve the goal of creating the "skills army." A disaster G.I. Bill can be set up for people who served in a disaster recovery effort and need a stipend to learn a skilled trade. Volunteers learn what skilled jobs are possible from first responders. A government/business consortium builds on this momentum and provides help. The new army of skilled workers turns disaster into prosperity.

Good Use For Closed Military Bases

Submitted by Heather H. in Illinois

Recently we have gone through a round of military base-closings. During the same period we have experienced the most devastating hurricane in U.S. history. One big problem was the lack of places to put dislocated victims. Another was the lack of coordination getting in supplies and medicine. I propose that we turn over several of these bases to the emergency management people and that they be retooled and maintained as national disaster centers. We could store emergency supplies in these places and fly supplies to disaster areas or fly/drive victims to the ex-bases to be temporarily housed. If we had one center for each area of the country and more for areas likely to experience natural disasters, we wouldn't be so uncoordinated in our response to disasters.

Ration Gas
Submitted by anonymous in Washington

The Problem:
Diminishing oil supplies worldwide mean America is running out of cheap oil.

International trade is out of balance as our dependence on imported oil increases.

The Solution:

Let our free market economy work for all of us by rationing gasoline. Allow every man/woman/child a set amount of gas per week/month and issue ration cards for that amount. Allow people to sell or barter their rationed limit to others. People would either learn to live within their limits or pay what the "market" makes available.

The Benefit:

- More people using mass transportation/car pooling.
- People driving more efficiently (55-60 miles per hour).
- More sales of fuel-efficient automobiles.
- Share the wealth; the more affluent can pay those without autos for their ration cards.

The Result:

- More product research and development of alternative fuels.
- Less dependence on imported oil.
- Less pollution.
- A stronger economy.

Survivor: Congress Edition
Submitted by Eileen T. in District Of Columbia

Every Senator and Representative should be challenged to live within an average American family's budget for one month and figure out how to get all the essentials—housing, food, clothing, health care, child care, utilities, education, and all the other essentials of life—without going into debt or getting assistance from government-provided social programs (Medicaid, food stamps, etc.) AND have enough to save for college and retirement.

An average percentage of the participating Members of Congress would also have to live without health care insurance, just like the 46 million Americans who do it every day.

While living like a typical American family for one month is by no means the same as what we do every day, participating in such an experiment might make a Senator or Representative pause and think about his or her decisions differently when they are debating cuts to vital programs to pay for a growing deficit that is fueled mainly by the costs of war and huge tax breaks for the super rich.

Credit Card Mania
Submitted by Tina M. B. in Massachusetts

The Problem:

The over-issuance of credit cards by financial/retail institutions is the catalyst to individual abuse and mounting personal and national debt.

The Fix:
- Create a 'watch-dog' organization consisting of financial, retail, and cardholder representatives.
- Tighten the general criteria (i.e. income, job longevity, limit) for credit card offerings.
- Tighten mechanisms for sharing of mailing lists for potential cardholders and bulk mailing offerings.
- Reduce special promotions (i.e. frequent-flyer points with purchases, money back on purchases, discounts).
- Reduce, if not eliminate, 'pre-approved' credit card offerings.
- Develop 'affordable' credit card programs specifically designed for first-time holders or holders who are rebuilding their credit.
- Develop minimal 'interest' bearing credit cards for medical-related expenses with deferment options for those qualifying.
- Require financial institutions making credit card offerings to develop and offer optional and mandatory education on credit card usage.

The Benefits:
- Increase available cash.
- Decrease 'high' monthly payments.
- Decrease interest paid.
- Decrease number of payees.
- Decrease debt.
- Decrease bankruptcy filings.
- Increase principal payment.
- Increase family harmony.
- Decrease the financial organizations' bad-debt ratios.

International Minimum Wage
Submitted by Carlos H. in Washington

Problem: Jobs being outsourced to the lowest bidder.

Solution: An international minimum wage that all international businesses must follow.

How it works: By having international stability in labor costs, businesses will consider other factors when determining where to produce goods. These factors may include the regional economy, taxes, and quality of the workforce. When these factors are considered, jobs will more likely stay in the U.S. Also, labor-cost stability will be good for the bottom line and the average American stockholder.

Currently, jobs leave the U.S., go to Mexico, then China, then Vietnam, and onward as each nation undercuts the last. This pattern leaves behind a trail of "ghost towns." By putting a stop to this, the U.S. will experience the benefits above and also help limit global poverty. Limiting global poverty will help prevent everything from immigration problems to the spread of disease to terrorism.

The minimum wage works in the U.S. and can work for the world if the wage is low enough. We should lobby the World Trade Organization, World Bank, and the United Nations.

Household Energy Monitor
Submitted by Richard R. in California

I am sure I am not the only person to have opened the electric bill and been confronted with sticker shock. "How did I use THAT much electricity??"

I propose a simple device installed in the home that will monitor household electrical usage. The device could display current usage, average usage, and project the monthly bill based on current kilowatt cost. The device could also warn the user when the projected bill will exceed a pre-set threshold.

I have seen many great ideas for long-term energy solutions. These are all great ideas and many should be implemented. Use of this device, however, will reduce the monthly bill for the household now and widespread usage would result in less household energy usage nationwide.

More Public Health Clinics And Doctors
Submitted by John F. in Florida

The national debate over affordable health insurance needs to change into a debate on how to provide affordable health care to more Americans.

The Idea:

Create a large-scale public program to recruit medical school students into public service at new public health care clinics.

Like the military model, medical school tuition could be paid for in exchange for a certain number of years of public service. Not only would large-scale public delivery of health care

Photos by Earl Dotter.

service result in increased access to primary care for America's uninsured, it would also reduce the debt our medical students face when leaving medical school for private practice.

Most importantly, the availability of public health clinics on a large scale would make primary health care available much more affordably than the current delivery through our nation's hospital emergency rooms.

Public health clinics and public health doctors should not replace the current private delivery mechanisms, but supplement them for Americans who aren't insured or insurable.

Health care costs are spiraling out of control. Public, not-for-profit solutions should be considered.

Work To Learn
Submitted by Jackie S. in Illinois

The Problem: Affording college.

The Solution: High school kids would start working now in entry-level positions for governmental and nonprofit agencies to earn credits towards college. The hours would be restricted so as to not conflict with school and the tasks would be tailored towards the person's interests. This way, the students would get a bit of real-world experience before choosing a major in college and possibly be more certain about the direction they would like their lives to take.

The Benefits: Not only does it teach kids accountability, but it will spare them an enormous student loan burden as well as make them appreciate the college experience all the more, knowing how hard they had to work to be there.

Reimburse Top 5% Of Graduates
Submitted by Douglas R. in Missouri

The federal government should have a full reimbursement of educational tuition and room and board for the top 5% of all undergraduate and graduate students in approved areas of study required in the labor market as determined by the U.S. Department of Labor, Bureau of Labor Statistics, or a combination of sources. For instance, if there is a shortage of electrical engineers, then the top 5% of degree earners (undergrad and grad) in this discipline will be fully reimbursed.

Of course, there would need to be stringent guidelines and the Arts would be categorized as a necessary discipline, since the health of any progressive nation requires a thriving artistic/cultural landscape. This would benefit working families, because it would give incentives to students to perform well in needed skill sets in higher learning, which would lead to greater career opportunities. It would also allow graduates to begin contributing to driving the economic engine by having disposable income sooner after graduation, and reduce some portion of the "debtor nation" syndrome.

Bus Service In Rural Areas
Submitted by Neil S. in Nevada

We have large rural areas in the United States that have people who live there with no transportation of their own, with no way to get to metropolitan areas for medical, dental, and especially medical specialists' service.

We could use local school buses to make trips to metropolitan areas for medical and dental needs, business, shopping, visiting friends, and relatives, etc.

We could pick up other passengers at other pick-up points along the way. This could be organized over the Internet. You would have passengers make reservations, and the driver would collect the fares the day of the trip.

There could be weekend trips to all kinds of events, parades, fairs, sports events, scenic trips, etc. These could be open to everyone in the community. People would spend money on food, shopping, gifts, etc. This would put people to work in service and manufacturing jobs.

The school buses could be used to connect with national bus lines, charter buses, Amtrak, airlines, etc. They would pick passengers up when they return.

Outsourced Jobs Help Fund Social Security
Submitted by Michael B. in Colorado

The problem of outsourcing jobs not only leaves working people scrambling to find new (and oftentimes lower-paying) jobs, it also reduces the funds that go into the Social Security trust fund.

While we may not be able to stop outsourcing, we can at least make it less desirable by requiring corporations that outsource jobs to do the following: Require that for each overseas worker a corporation employs, the corporation pays into the Social Security trust fund the same amount that worker would pay into the system were he/she in the U.S.

This would make outsourcing less desirable to corporations and also help support the solvency of the Social Security trust fund.

Savings Bonds At Check-Out Counters
Submitted by Katherine Y. in Tennessee

Americans do not save enough to fund their retirement, or to tide them over in short-term economic crises. For many people, saving for retirement seems to be an overwhelming task that is scary to even contemplate. For others, they do not have a bank account, or have difficulty getting to the bank due to work schedules. We have to make it easier for Americans to save. The U.S. government should offer savings bonds at check-out counters, just like the gift cards that all retailers offer now. Right now, it is too difficult to buy a U.S. savings bond. There is technology available that would allow people to pay for a savings bond just like loading money on a gift card. People will easily be able to buy their own bond, or give a gift of a bond. A plastic card could be utilized for the bond. Retailers will have to be compensated just as lottery ticket sellers are compensated. This provides an easy, accessible, and fast way to get Americans saving again.

Narrow-Gauge Cars
Submitted by Mike S. in California

The Problems: Congested freeways. High cost of gas. Air pollution. Declining U.S. automobile industry. High cost of freeway improvements. Dependence on foreign energy.

The Solution: Provide incentives for U.S. automakers to design a car narrow enough to fit two abreast in freeway lanes. These could be single or multi-passenger, but seating would be configured as single file. Initially allow these vehicles to use any regular lane of traffic, as well as carpool lanes, regardless of number of passengers. As the number of these vehicles increases, highway departments could re-stripe the #1 lanes of freeways as narrow-gauge use only.

The Benefits to Working Families: Shorter commute times, as there are effectively more lanes available. Reduced gas expenses, as most of these vehicles would likely weigh less than typical cars. Reduced air pollution. Reduced foreign energy dependence. Increased jobs, as the U.S. auto industry leads the world in this emerging field. Reduced highway taxes, as lane re-striping is far less expensive than land acquisition and new construction.

Uses existing technology. Easily implemented through legislation. Huge national benefits.

Not In My Back Yard
Submitted by anonymous in Washington

Not in my back yard (NIMBY).

The public rants and raves about crime, wants the government to do something about it, but doesn't want to pay for more jails. They want to lock criminals up, but do not want prisons located near them. They believe that treatment centers need to be available, but please, locate them somewhere far, far away.

So, let's do that. Build law and justice complexes in areas that need and want economic development. Plan prisons, with drug and alcohol treatment facilities included, in economically distressed areas where the population will welcome the jobs.

When locating these prison/treatment complexes, surround them with ancillary services that will also benefit the surrounding community. Such services might include:

- FBI, State Patrol, National Guard and military training centers.
- Wind-generating farms to supply energy needs.
- An animal refuge or grazing land.

The construction, maintenance, and operation of such facilities would offer an economic boost to the unemployed, provide programs that will result in less recidivism, and alleviate the NIMBY attitude.

Scooter Paths
Submitted by anonymous in Texas

Concern about rising fuel costs has many considering alternative transportation venues. Unfortunately, carpooling is not an option for some and many cities' mass transit systems are sorely lacking. Hence a growing interest in 'scooters'—one of the most effective transportation alternatives. Scooter commuters are vulnerable in traffic, however. Once scooters catch on so that demand justifies supply, we should create 'scooter paths' for these conservation-minded commuters.

Make Public Schools More Useful
Submitted by Dimitri C. in New York

Problem: School system out of date. Not everyone needs college.

Idea: Public school mandated through 10th grade, with option then of two years more in vocational school (skilled labor like mechanic or carpentry) or three years more academic track at junior college level (both options publicly funded). Must meet grade and behavior requirements to attend higher levels. Three-year track graduates require only two more years at a university for an undergraduate degree if a college degree is desired. In addition, federally mandate higher minimum teacher salaries in public schools to attract more people to teaching. There is no more important job than inspiring the young of the nation to be successful in their endeavors.

How it helps: It allows those who want to attend college to do so with only a two-year bill and cuts college costs. Provides useful track for 16 to 18-year-olds who prefer skilled labor jobs. Acknowledges that not everyone needs college. Attracts more and better teachers to schools. Allows for higher level of public education (using three-year academic track) than is currently available.

Rapid Train Travel Between Cities
Submitted by Richard M. in Arizona

The Problem: Suffocating travel time between close destinations.

To fix it, we need fast train systems between areas 500 miles apart or less. This would open more space up to thoughtful planning, affordable housing, and job creation along these routes. Europe excels; here we lag. We could develop state-of-the-art equipment here. Expertise at maintaining a whole new transportation system would benefit the economy, job creation, and job disbursement from core areas. Airports would handle capacity for much longer distances and money needed for improvements could go into building the train systems. Government help would be needed just like car and aviation are helped by budget expenditures. Imagine the ease of travel for all people as the travel of yesteryear becomes the travel of the future.

New Vision For American Development
Submitted by Garlynn W. in California

America today is dependent on foreign oil for transportation and foreign investment for the economy. To turn this around, I propose a new national transportation program, similar to the Interstate Highway System of the 1950s, centered around high-speed rail transportation corridor backbones, connecting to local commuter rail feeder lines.

New Transit-Oriented Development (TOD) would be centered around every station on the system, including a high density of mixed uses (residential, retail, office, live/work and business incubator spaces) that allow people to walk from home to work just as easily as they walk to the train station to get to the next town, the next state, or the other side of the continent. Construction of a national rail infrastructure system, including the high-speed main lines, would provide full employment for Americans in every region. After the initial transportation construction was completed, more employment would be provided in constructing the adjacent developments.

Finally, these developments would have many uses, providing employment, including business incubators to grow the economy. It's just the right thing to do.

The University of America
Submitted by Dane G. in Florida

Create "The University of America" on campuses across the country. The initial campuses could be set up on closed military bases. These properties already have family and dormitory housing, classrooms, medical clinics or hospitals, and often elementary schools and recreational facilities. Other campuses could be built later if needed.

Anyone already receiving, or eligible for, public assistance could enroll. Students (and/or family members living with them) would be required to help staff day care, clinics, supervise playgrounds, etc. for a few hours a week in addition to attending classes. High school/GED, college, and vocational/technical training would be available. Since most necessities are provided, students would receive a small stipend and then transitional assistance upon graduation.

The university system would be administered via a trust set up by Congress and administered by a board of regents—half appointed by Congress and half by the President.

Providing these students a safe environment to acquire a first-rate higher education would benefit all Americans with more educated and hopeful citizens while saving billions of dollars.

Water Everywhere But Not To Drink
Submitted by Dale F. in Kansas

Three-fourths of the planet is water and many of humanity's problems are the result of droughts and shortages. We need more research in desalination, pipelines, and agriculture that can tolerate small amounts of salt. With an abundance of "cropland water" available to irrigate arid lands, there would be plenty of crops suitable for ethanol, biofuels, and maybe even livestock and human feed. Eventually, reverse osmosis, or some other process, would finish the job on the "cropland water" and turn it into "fresh water." Adequate water everywhere in the world could certainly solve a lot of problems.

Consolidate Small Midwest Towns
Submitted by William F. in Kansas

Kansas, Nebraska, and many other states have large sparsely populated areas. The small towns in these areas are disappearing at an alarming rate. The nation needs these areas to prosper so that basic and modern needs can be supplied to the existing and future local farmers and ranchers.

Create new towns that are strategically located. These new towns will consolidate several of the existing towns that are too small to survive as is. They will have modern, well-planned infrastructures, new schools, and combine the old businesses, populations and industry. Once the infrastructure is in place, the land would be free to the "homesteaders." The government would purchase the obsolete property so that seed money would be available to those who would relocate to the new town.

The U.S. would not only sustain, but would greatly stimulate the agricultural community. These towns would be a Mecca for those in search of a better life. New industry would locate there so as to take advantage of this great new opportunity.

Saving Social Security
Submitted by Dennis L. in New Mexico

To keep Social Security solvent for generations, we must eliminate the salary cap on the FICA tax. When you consider that instead of collecting about $52,500 from the top ten salaries of CEOs, for example, we (I say "we" because WE are the government, remember) would collect more than $30 million a year. Now add all the other million-dollar salaries and we're in pretty good shape.

But you have to impose a cap on payments, because we don't want a situation where we're paying retired multi-millionaires millions in Social Security benefits.

Come on, rich folks, how greedy can you be? This change would put no significant dent in your massive fortunes.

Reduce Workweek And Commuting
Submitted by Gregory W. in California

We need a new standard: a four-day, 36-hour workweek, with one-fifth less commuting.

A new government-defined, standard 36-hour working week of four nine-hour days would reduce the workweek by one-tenth while reducing commuting, which in America is a fast-growing form of dangerous and fatiguing unpaid work.

This would be a time- and money-saving boon for workers who would like to work this way and for their families—while greatly reducing stressful and time-wasting traffic congestion, use of gasoline, carbon dioxide emissions, and public and personal costs of all kinds.

These four nine-hour days should be non-consecutive as much as possible. For example, you could work Monday-to-Tuesday and then Thursday-to-Friday, or Tuesday-to-Thursday and then Saturday.

This definitive redefinition of the 40-hour workweek to a new 36-hour standard workweek would also create the space for more job creation. This reform also would increase American per-hour productivity, a phenomenon definitively demonstrated in Europe.

From this, we can go on to establish a new 32-hour workweek of four eight-hour days! Isn't this what our fine technology was developed for?

Fixing Social Security
Submitted by anonymous in Ohio

The Problem: Social Security.

The Explanation/Solution: Social Security in this country is headed for big trouble. Congress has been slow to respond to fixing it, partly because Members of Congress have their own separate retirement system. If Congress abolished its own extremely lucrative pension plan and was forced to use the same system as the common folk, we'd have Social Security fixed in no time.

The Benefit: Having a reliable Social Security program in place will help secure the future welfare of the American people.

Prepaid Future Card To Help Economy
Submitted by Scott C. in New Jersey

The Problems: 1) Savings accounts offer low returns on investment; and 2) businesses face challenges trying to grow.

The Solution: An interest-bearing, business-branded "Future-Card." It's a gift card that sells for less than its face value and matures to face value at a pre-set date in the future.

Stores use future discounts as a form of interest. A $20.00 Future-Card could sell for $16.00 and be worth $16.00, but matures to $20.00 in six months or a year from activation. The store is not offering 20% off. They are giving that consumer a 25% return.

Stores benefit by securing consumers, breakage, lift, float, and the ability to project sales.

Buy for others as a gift card for next year. Buy at your grocery store or places you frequently shop. Use with other coupons. It's a cash card. Consumers invest in business and get more interest than a savings account.

I buy $200.00 in groceries each week. $800.00 now would be $1000.00 next year? That's a 25% return.

Tax Break For Debt Reduction
Submitted by anonymous in Illinois

Credit card debt is an enormous problem for working Americans. Two incomes are often needed to service family debt. Without a savings cushion, any unexpected expense results in increased debt, and job loss can lead to bankruptcy.

The Credit Reform Act passed in 2005 was a boon to creditors who were already reaping record profits. Working Americans deserve at least as much help.

My solution is to reform the tax code to again make consumer interest deductible, but only if taxpayers apply any refund to their credit card debt. Refunds would be direct-deposited to account numbers supplied by the taxpayer. The combination of extra cash and direct deposit would accelerate debt repayment. This provision should apply to all taxpayers, regardless of income.

The reduction of consumer debt will help families increase their standard of living, even without earning additional money. Families can build savings and make decisions based on family goals and values, not out of the need to eliminate debt.

Make Amtrak A Biodiesel Innovator
Submitted by anonymous in Washington

America needs to lessen dependency on foreign oil, help farmers, and have a redundant transportation system. Do this by fully funding an expanded Amtrak long-distance train system and requiring that all non-electric locomotives and Amtrak Thruway buses be powered by biodiesel.

The Benefits:
A. Establishes a large market for biodiesel, thus lowering the cost for ordinary users.
B. Provides a robust surface transportation network, using a mode Americans know and like.
C. Provides living-wage union jobs for average Americans.
D. Provides transit to rural areas that are lacking it since Greyhound and the airlines have cut back service.
E. Benefits American farmers who grow the soybeans that are used to create biodiesel.
F. Ensures mobility for disabled Americans.
G. Encourages the most eco-friendly transportation mode.

Railroads that host Amtrak trains could be given money to maintain the right-of-way that the Amtrak trains run on, thus helping improve the national infrastructure.

Funding would come from the existing gas tax revenues. By creating a dedicated fund, it will take Amtrak off the annual politically motivated funding drama.

Solarize Our Schools
Submitted by William M. in California

I teach in a large high school in south Los Angeles. We have a number of large buildings and a couple of blank walls with southern exposures. What would happen if we installed state-of-the-art solar energy panels on the roofs of my school? With the advent of nanotechnology, we could even put solar energy collectors on parts of our walls. With solar-energy collectors on the school site, we could cut our energy bills. Since much of my school is shut down for the summer, at the time of peak electricity demand, we could sell our surplus energy. We could use the proceeds from this energy sale for the school. It would be sort of like having an oil well on the premises. Solarizing schools in Los Angeles—installing solar energy collectors wherever possible—would jump start the solar-energy sector. It would reduce our dependence on fossil fuels and every working family in America would benefit.

FOCUS On Poverty
Submitted by Geoffrey G. in North Carolina

Too many working families in America live below the poverty line. This would end with my concept, FOCUS: Food, Clothing, Housing and Health-care Assistance to Working Families in the U.S.

The program could be financed in a way that is both tax- and deficit-neutral, in part by raising the minimum wage by $2 over the course of a four-year Presidential term. The remaining funds would come from making bold decisions to re-order priorities in the existing federal budget. The latter would entail cutting federal non-social discretionary spending by 50%. At the same time, the dignity of hard-working citizens could be preserved by allowing recipients both to apply for and to receive all assistance, including FOCUS benefits, at home. Americans who work hard do not have time to stand in long lines. FOCUS: Taking Care of America's Family Values.

Orphanages In Retirement Villages
Submitted by Pam V. in California

Problems: Unwanted children lost in the foster care system. Unwanted seniors alone and useless.

Solution: Re-introduce orphanages where children can live in a stable, consistent environment but add the one element that was always missing—loving grandparents! Instead of closing government military bases, convert them to retirement villages/orphanages. Today's active seniors and the aging baby-boomer generation have a lot to contribute, and would welcome the opportunity to play ball with a boy who has known nothing but abuse, or rock an AIDS baby to sleep.

How This Will Help Working Families: Raising happy productive children is usually the job of the family, but when a child or a senior does not have a family, why in the world don't we help them find each other?

Trade Corps
Submitted by Daniel L. in New York

21st Century American businesses should be given every advantage when bringing their products and services into the global marketplace. We invented the Peace Corps to help peoples overseas; AmeriCorps to strengthen our communities; now, to ensure the growth of our economy, it is time for a Trade Corps.

The Trade Corps would provide economic services to American businesses to better market and sell "Made in America" overseas, such as linkage to translators, cultural training, travel information, website design appropriate for particular countries, or arranging trade shows and presentations. Proactively, it would organize research databases for American companies to better approach and sell in individual overseas markets. If needed to troubleshoot, the Trade Corps could outline options and resources to resolve impasses.

A large segment of the organization's associates could be sponsored by private business. From affiliations and internships available to younger workers with fresh degrees yet seeking global experience, up to retirees with valuable wisdom, those in the Trade Corps would serve our nation overseas so our jobs grow back home.

Casting (Sliced) Bread Upon the Waters

By Amanda Levinson,
Director of Policy Programs, Hope Street Group

The past two decades have been a time of enormous change in our economy. Innovation in science, technology, and the global marketplace has increased consumer choices and possibilities, the overall wealth of our country has risen to historic levels, and many have benefited greatly from rising incomes, stock market prices, and home values. Yet there is also a widespread sense of unease about the state of the American Dream: a nagging sense that ordinary workers are working harder to keep up with their bills, that health care costs are eating deeper into paychecks, that families are going deeper in debt, that people's jobs and incomes are not as secure as they used to be, and that our children will need to learn much more, work much harder, and perhaps even be luckier in order to enjoy a more affluent lifestyle than their parents. Consider the following statistics:

- Household income volatility—the yearly amount that a household's inflation-adjusted income varies—has more than doubled since the early 1970s.

- The number of people living in poverty in America has increased over the last five years, from 31.6 million and 11.3 percent in 2000 to 37 million and 12.6 percent in 2005.

Since Sliced Bread *asked the Hope Street Group to highlight common themes emerging from the contest ideas. The Hope Street Group (www.hopestreetgroup.org) is a non-partisan, non-profit think tank of young business professionals dedicated to expanding economic opportunity and growth.*

- In 2001–02, an average of 13 million families spent 10 percent of family income on direct out-of-pocket health care expenses, according to a report from the Commonwealth Fund.

The majority of Americans still believes in the American Dream, and feels a responsibility to make that dream a reality for themselves and their families. At the same time, most Americans do not think that public policies, political leaders, or our government in general have kept pace with these changes to protect and deepen the dream of increasing prosperity and expanding opportunity for all. According to surveys, only 34% think the country is generally "on the right track." And the last Congress had an approval rating in 2006 of a mere 27%—the lowest it's been since 1994. Nor are people more confident in business, the media, or other institutions to reflect their values and work for their interests.

It is in this context that the **Since Sliced Bread** competition was launched by the SEIU. The explicit goal of **Since Sliced Bread** was to solicit ideas from ordinary Americans that would improve the lives of working people and strengthen our economy. What emerged from this contest was a national brainstorm of ideas in every conceivable category of public policy—from alternative energy, health care, immigration reform, and international trade to personal debt, jobs, and the environment. The outpouring of ideas not only shatters the myth that Americans don't care about policy, but also shows that average Americans are thinking broadly and creatively about the issues that have a daily impact on their lives.

SEIU recently asked Hope Street Group, a non-partisan, non-profit organization of young business professionals dedicated to promoting an Opportunity Economy (policies that expand economic opportunity in a high-growth economy) to review the ideas coming out of **Since Sliced Bread** with an eye to revealing the common themes and concerns that Americans share. You can learn more about Hope Street Group and how **Since Sliced Bread** solutions reflect the principles of creating an Opportunity Economy at Hope Street Group's website (www.hopestreetgroup.org). We found many innovative and generous ideas on the **Since Sliced Bread** website that promote economic opportunity. We also found that Americans share remarkably similar concerns and values.

Transcending the Red State/Blue State Divide:
A New Role for Government
in Achieving the American Dream

Since **Sliced Bread** should dispel any doubts that Americans share concerns about the most pressing issues facing them in today's economy. The more than 22,000 ideas came from every congressional district in the nation—a veritable map that policy-makers should read to get a sense of what's on the minds of ordinary Americans today.

The concerns raised on the **Since Sliced Bread** website went beyond the red state/blue state binary that many would have us believe determines the day-to-day lives of ordinary Americans. Thousands of people, from South Dakota to New York, Arkansas to California, wrote in with trepidations and hopes that transcend this imaginary divide. By and large, Americans are concerned with creating jobs, fixing health care and education, finding alternative ways to become energy efficient, building homeownership, relieving personal debt and increasing assets, and securing retirement no matter where they live or whom they vote for.

And yet, the surprising finding was in the number of **Since Sliced Bread** ideas that reflected both a skeptical attitude towards the government's ability to solve America's problems, while at the same time proposing the expansion or creation of new government programs to resolve these same issues. This apparent contradiction is understandable. Some of the ideas proposed that government take a direct hand in solving the problems identified, such as massive public works projects to boost employment. But more of the ideas looked to government to provide incentives for businesses, to invest in people's skills, and to provide access to markets and opportunities. The vast majority of proposals showed Americans reaching for solutions that will empower and engage individuals, families, communities, and businesses supported by a government that is more innovative, productive, and responsive to the aspirations of ordinary people.

Since Sliced Bread's top prize-winners offer excellent examples of proposals that retool government's role in the lives of ordinary citizens. Peter Skidmore won the contest's top prize with his idea to create locally-owned sustainable resource industries through funds generated by taxes on pollution, development, and fossil fuels. By using funds generated by taxation to fund renewable energy and environmental restoration, Peter envisions a role for government that simultaneously supports new avenues of job growth and alternative energy technologies.

Contest runner-up Filippo Menczer's proposal to tie the minimum wage to the Cost-of-Living Index abolishes the politicians' role altogether in setting the minimum wage. Letting cost of living determine the minimum wage eliminates the need for the bitter political battle that drains the time our lawmakers could be spending on other issues.

Leslie Hester, the other contest runner-up, revamps the critical role government plays in funding public education. She proposes to equitably fund all public schools through redirecting local property taxes into a general state fund. Combined with her ideas to control tuition at public universities and increase teacher salaries, Leslie upgrades the important role government can play in improving the chance for every American to have access to affordable, quality education.

A similar revisioning of government's role in the lives of citizens can be seen in other topics addressed by contest participants:

- Finalist Susan Almeida proposes to support job and business creation by creating an agency that would allow small- and medium-sized businesses to get capital from local funders (idea # 18218).

- Martin Johnson, who was a Top 21 winner, proposes establishing universal access to health care by creating digital records to reduce paperwork and starting a gradual single-payer health care system for adults under 35 (idea # 412).

- John F. of Florida suggests creating more public health clinics staffed by recent medical school graduates who would work there in exchange for loan forgiveness (idea #9945).

- Susan C. in Florida's idea—to create individual pre-tax educational accounts for people to tap into in order to gain new skills and training throughout their lives—tackles the need for workers to learn new skills in our rapidly evolving economy (idea # 16062).

What is remarkable about these ideas is their shared conviction that government should be a catalyst for—rather than the sole proprietor of—programs and initiatives that expand economic self-sufficiency and growth.

Common Concerns, Shared Dreams: A Sampling of Themes Emerging from **Since Sliced Bread**

Since **Sliced Bread** provided a powerful interactive platform for Americans to debate and discuss what matters most in their lives. Underpinning the thousands of ideas submitted to the contest lies a deep, shared desire to achieve the American Dream—good-paying jobs, access to health care, education, homeownership, retirement, and a better life for our children and grandchildren. And although there was lively debate about the best ways to implement the ideas, from topic to topic the articulation of what needs fixing was remarkably similar.

Creating more and better jobs:

Anonymous in Maryland writes, "Today, small business is the engine that drives the American economy, creating the majority of new jobs and innovations" (idea # 18067). A big part of the American dream is starting a business, and many in the contest see new business creation as a way to help replenish jobs lost to outsourcing. But contest participants realize that small business owners need a boost to help get them off the ground, and so ideas abounded about how to support new businesses and encourage job creation.

Fixing health care:

On the topic of health care, Kathern B. from Tennessee writes, "My issue and problem is health care in America today. Whether it be in the workplace or private sector, it affects every person, business, owner, and employee. Millions are without this necessity. America, we can do better!" (idea #23106). With the rising costs of health care straining the average American's pocketbook, thousands of **Since Sliced Bread** participants wrote in with their ideas to cut the costs of—and increase access to—health care.

Improving education:

Diane F. in Michigan writes, "Each generation should have a better quality of life than the one before it. Every American should have equal access to higher education. The cost of a college education has skyrocketed to the point where it is almost out of reach for the middle and lower classes" (idea # 22010). This is a sentiment shared by many participants. Americans are clearly concerned with the cost, accessibility, and quality of education. The sense that our children—and adults—must be better prepared to compete in the global economy was also a recurring theme throughout the contest.

Increasing sources of alternative energy:

The concern about America's dependence on foreign oil and the rising cost of energy was raised by thousands of contestants. As Brad R. in Florida writes, "In my opinion energy is first and foremost the most important issue facing our country today. Our country uses millions of barrels of oil everyday and we depend on other countries to supply it to us. We have the knowledge and means to develop alternative types of fuel that could power anything from automobile engines to power plants" (idea # 23044). Many people like Brad were optimistic that despite our energy troubles, America has the know-how and the resources to generate alternative sources of energy.

Increasing homeownership:

"The American Dream is for everyone to have an equal opportunity to live in peace and get a home for their families," writes David G. of Virginia (idea #22479). Many **Since Sliced Bread** participants see owning homes as an important leg up to the middle class, but worry that dream is increasingly out of reach due to rising housing costs and the lack of assets. Creative solutions to helping more Americans become homeowners featured prominently in the contest ideas.

Ensuring retirement for everybody:

Anonymous in California had this to say about the current state of retirement benefits in America: "Retirement benefits for most working Americans are anything but secure. Additionally, a substantial portion of the workforce, especially the younger generations, expect and prefer to jump from job to job as their skill-base increases; this trend will undoubtedly further stress pension funds at major corporations" (idea # 8707). With anxiety running high about the future of retirement benefits, many people offered up creative solutions on how to prepare for retirement.

Relieving personal debt and increasing assets:

"What is the American Dream?" asks Anita C. of Florida. "Is it to live a good life and be happy? To get married and raise a family, to be able to live a life without an everyday struggle, or just to one day own a home? I believe it's all the above. In order to save the U.S. economy, we must first teach the people in our economy how to save" (idea # 23049). Spiraling personal debt, a lack of understanding of financial management, and an inability to save for the future were all on the minds of people who wrote into **Since Sliced Bread**. Without savings, the American Dream will remain out of reach for millions.

Public Policy by the People, for the People: The **Since Sliced Bread** Folksonomy

The thousands of submissions to **Since Sliced Bread** are nothing less than astonishing, upending the common wisdom that says ordinary Americans are apathetic when it comes to policy debate. On the contrary, these ideas are as much a gauge of what concerns ordinary Americans as they are a powerful illustration of the untapped potential for policy participation and debate that exists at the grassroots. You can visit Hope Street Group's website (www.hopestreetgroup.org) for a discussion of how ideas like those on **Since Sliced Bread** can expand economic opportunity and growth.

The SEIU has unveiled another ambitious phase of **Since Sliced Bread,** asking the American public to sort and rank the thousands of ideas submitted to the contest. We hope you will join **Since Sliced Bread** in its second phase as a "folksonomy." As the public looks at this dizzying range of ideas across many different topics, we should keep in mind that we now have a unique opportunity to participate in building a grassroots policy movement. Which ideas will have the greatest positive impact on working families? Which ideas will help us grow a strong economy for our children's future? Public policy by the people, for the people is a tall order, but Americans are clearly ready to take center stage in the roles that will determine our future.

It's now up to all of us to keep these ideas—and the American Dream—alive.

American Dreamers
*Since Sliced Bread and
the Opportunity Economy*

By The Hope Street Group

Recently, the Service Employees International Union (SEIU) challenged ordinary Americans to submit their best idea "**Since Sliced Bread**" on how to strengthen the economy and improve the lives of working Americans and their families. In a testament to the vitality of civic America, over 22,000 responses poured in from every congressional district in the country—and from every geography, political affiliation, age, and socioeconomic background.

The SEIU turned to Hope Street Group to provide a thematic assessment of this extraordinary avalanche of ideas. Hope Street Group leaders and members embraced this challenge because we believe that bold, innovative solutions are urgently needed to transcend the polarized debate in Washington and create a consensus on how to expand growth and opportunity in today's dynamic global economy. We were honored to help with the Since Sliced Bread contest's unusually innovative approach for bringing the "kitchen table" ideas of ordinary Americans into the public debate. Hope Street Group volunteers from all over the country offered their time to review hundreds of submissions, and Hope Street Group wrote an essay (pp. 128-134) discussing the common hopes and concerns that emerged from the contest.

In this essay, we aim to build on the contributions of the **Since Sliced Bread** contestants by proposing a framework for how Americans should think about opportunity and prosperity.

The contest itself begged the question, "How well can we achieve the American Dream at a time of enormous economic, social, and political transformation?" Americans seem to think that we need to update the approaches our parents and grandparents relied on to achieve this dream. While the **Since Sliced Bread** contestants were resoundingly clear on their most important hopes and concerns, they were much more conflicted on the best tactics for realizing their goals. Is it through new government programs? Is it through new regulations or mandates on business? Is it through a mix of incentives and market-based solutions? Is it through citizen action and volunteerism? The contestants proposed ideas using all of these methods, and more.

In this essay, we aim to integrate the ideas proposed by **Since Sliced Bread** into the national policy debate on increasing economic opportunity and prosperity by proposing a framework for our public policy debates that keeps the concerns revealed by the contest front and center, while building a more integrated set of solutions.

Hope Street Group is uniquely positioned to build on these papers to suggest a robust approach for reviving the American Dream. As a nonpartisan, nonprofit organization of young business professionals dedicated to expanding economic opportunity in a high-growth economy—what we refer to as an "Opportunity Economy" —we are always looking for bold, innovative solutions that will help our country achieve those goals. In an Opportunity Economy, people are encouraged to take risks to invest in themselves and their families, and to better their condition. Opportunity Economics solutions, which Hope Street Group develops and promotes, are aimed at 'operationalizing' the American Dream in the 21st century.

The remainder of this essay presents the underlying elements of an Opportunity Economy, and shows how the **Since Sliced Bread** ideas fit into that larger framework.

Oiling the Gears of the American Dream Machine: Putting the Best Ideas **Since Sliced Bread** into Action

America's economy at the start of the 21st century is undergoing dynamic changes in response to global forces, changes that are creating both tremendous opportunities and challenges for American workers. While job growth in the low- and high-skilled sectors is expanding, middle-class jobs are becoming increasingly scarce. Returns to human capital are rising, and yet many of our youth are finding education unequal and inadequate for the high-skilled jobs being created. Returns to assets are also rising, but access to markets remains highly unequal. And household income volatility—the yearly amount that a household's inflation-adjusted income varies—has more than doubled since the early 1970s. In addition, short-sighted political reaction to such uncertainty risks stifling the competitive environment that is most responsible for rising productivity and per capita income. In short, the American Dream—that with hard work one's family can achieve upward mobility and a middle-class life—is becoming increasingly out of reach for millions of Americans. In plainer language, these realities and concerns surface again and again in the concerns raised and ideas proposed by **Since Sliced Bread** contestants.

So, how can the best ideas **Since Sliced Bread** be put into action? How can we tune up "the American Dream Machine" for the 21st century? How can we build the Opportunity Economy that so many of the **Since Sliced Bread** contestants were trying to describe? How can we harness the forces of innovation and competition that generate economic growth in tandem with the systematic expansion of opportunity to all Americans? In order to re-tool the American Dream, Hope Street Group embraces six themes that cut across specific issue areas such as health care or jobs or housing, and many **Since Sliced Bread** ideas reflected these six themes of an Opportunity Economy:

THE OPPORTUNITY ECONOMICS VISION – BUILDING A BROAD-BASED OPPORTUNITY ECONOMY FOR 21ST CENTURY COMPETITION

Opportunity Economy
- Equality of opportunity
- High-growth economy
- Mutually reinforcing policies

☐ Opportunity economics agenda

Level playing field capitalism – "Access for all to the power of markets"
- Broad-based access to markets – labor, capital, credit, housing, products/services
- Low barriers to business competition, innovation, and productivity growth
- Fiscal balance and low inflation – intergenerational fairness

Prosperity escalators	Human capital gains	Social trampoline
"Working families building earning power and assets"	**"A fair start for all Americans; capital that can't be taken away"**	**"Everyone can take risks and get a second chance"**
• Robust and flexible labor – more entry-level jobs	• Universal kindergarten readiness	• Universal/portable/flexible pensions and full retirement security
• Progressive tax system – low "entry level" taxes on workers	• Raising K-12 standards and closing socio-economic achievement gap	• Universal/portable/accessible health care (e.g., preventive, children's, catastrophic)
• Universal savings and affordable entry-level home ownership	• Highly accessible college and continuing adult education	• Robust worker retraining and welfare-to-work support
	• High professionalism, innovation, and pay in teaching profession	

Modernizing government – "Public goods improve as fast as private goods"
- Policy innovation to expand economic opportunity and productivity
- Public investment in market infrastructure and basic science
- Continuous productivity improvement in delivering government services

Social trust and engagement – "We're all in it together and each doing our share"
- Strong families and local communities – family-friendly public policies
- Vibrant voluntary institutions (e.g., faith-based, civic associations, unions) and civic engagement
- National defense and international engagement
- Universal public safety and systematic crime reduction

Level Playing Field Capitalism:
"Access for all to the power of markets"

In order for our economy to meet the rising expectations implicit in the American Dream, innovation and competition must allow more consumer choices and higher productivity, year after year. Everyone must have a chance to participate in that market dynamism. Returns on investments—in new equipment, new technology, new workers, an education, a new home—will be widely accessible and not be undermined by excessive inflation or government borrowing.

Underlying most of the **Since Sliced Bread** ideas was a commitment to the value of hard work and the understanding that competing in markets creates wealth, choice, and opportunities. Many of the ideas focused on giving people who do not have full access to markets a more level playing field. For example:

- David Y. of Indiana had the idea to create jobs and spur economic growth in inner cities through a program that would give derelict or abandoned properties tax-free for five years to people to be able to start businesses. Potential business owners would also be given low-interest loans to help offset the costs of starting a new business (idea #19004).

- Iona F. of North Carolina promotes growing America's small businesses through her idea of exempting small businesses from sales and use taxes during their first four months, having three months of small-business tax-exemption per year, and giving any business that expands after three years special earned credit on taxes (idea #22562).

- Top 21 winner Diana Nolen wants to integrate personal financial management into the school curriculum beginning in first grade and continuing through high school (idea #10140).

Prosperity Escalators:
"Working families building earning power and assets"

In an Opportunity Economy, young families and entry-level workers can climb the ladder of success, through hard work, thrift, and persistence. Public policies that increase the earning power, take-home pay, savings, and assets of working families are essential to maintaining the reality of the American Dream. An enormous number of **Since Sliced Bread** proposals touched on some 'prosperity escalator' idea, particularly with reference to helping people to own their own homes and increase savings. Some example ideas:

- Jay W. of Alabama proposed that a portion of the money low-income families pay in rent to public housing be made available to them to purchase a home after a few years (idea #19282).

- Robert F. of Florida's idea is to allow certain first-time homeowners a fixed-rate mortgage rather than one with compound interest, which would allow younger and low-income individuals and families to purchase a home (idea #23018).

- Melanie Jones of Indiana's winning idea for creating more low-income homeowners is to encourage them to purchase abandoned houses through a low-interest mortgage program (idea #10404).

- Anonymous of Wisconsin recommends that the U.S. government help give individuals a boost on saving for retirement by depositing $1,000 into a Social Security account to accrue interest for every newborn citizen throughout his or her lifetime (idea # 222).

If given real access to markets—whether to jobs, homes, business ownership, or financial assets—and the tools to compete in them, most ordinary Americans will seize that opportunity and expand the circle of innovation and competition to the benefit of our whole economy.

Human Capital Gains:
"A fair start for all Americans; capital you can't lose"

At the beginning of the 20th century, it was ownership of financial capital—stocks, bonds, and land—that separated the prosperous from "the rest of us." Now at the beginning of the 21st century, in a far wealthier country, it is human capital—educational attainment, professional expertise, credentials, networks, and connections—that is critical to ensure that all children are equipped to participate in our society, and that adults have the skills required by our dynamic economy. The idea that every American should have a fair start at a chance to compete in life—is a compelling moral responsibility echoed in many ideas submitted to **Since Sliced Bread**:

- Hillary M. of Michigan proposes to offer state-funded preschool to every child between the ages of 3 and 5 through the public school system, suggesting that the cost of adding two new grades to the school system would be offset by the productivity of caregivers returning to the workforce (idea #21659).

- Cindy M. of Texas recommends providing every low-income apartment complex with a Toddler Intervention Program, which would have a literacy program and teach parents good nutrition and parenting skills (idea #21963).

- Steven S. in Oregon suggests defraying the cost of higher education and motivating students to work harder in high school by providing scholarship money to students who score high on Advanced Placement (AP) exams (idea #20794).

In the 21st century knowledge-intensive economy, with returns to human capital rising, we can only begin to approximate equality of opportunity when high quality pre-kindergarten, K-12 education, access to college and advanced vocational training are widely available.

Social Trampoline:
"Everyone can take risks and get a second chance"

Ingrained in the idea of the American Dream is the belief that everybody should get a second chance: whether a person faces unemployment because they were laid off when their company lost out to new technology or competition, or had to stop working to care for a family member. Americans need policies that will allow them to bounce back from setbacks. We also need policies that reflect the reality of a dynamic economy, that do not increase the costs of losing a job, or discourage workers from changing jobs or starting their own small businesses by tying health care benefits and pensions to specific employers. Portable and flexible pensions, retirement funds, and health care accounts, as well as robust worker retraining in the face of downsizing and outsourcing, are just some of the ideas submitted to **Since Sliced Bread:**

- Ruth U. in Massachusetts proposes that every employer be required to pay a certain percentage of an employee's salary into a centrally managed pension fund, so that workers could continue to accrue retirement funds even if they change jobs (idea #22634).

- John Biddle, whose idea made him a contest finalist, wants retirement assets to be owned and controlled by the worker. His proposal would allow any employee who chose to do so to allocate retirement funds into an individual retirement account (idea #3714).

- Brynne V. in Florida has an innovative solution for worker retraining following a layoff: focus retraining efforts on the skills needed to operate a small business; offer workers training in management, finance and marketing; and provide workers with low-interest loans, tax breaks, grants and the option to pool their resources and form cooperatives (idea #20304).

Even as the volatility of the economy has increased, millions of well-paid, well-educated U.S. workers regularly take risks—starting businesses, going back to school, seeking a new job—to invest in themselves, and reap great rewards. Social trampoline policies for the 21st century will allow ordinary workers and families the freedom and security to realize their own full potential.

Modernizing Government:
"Public goods improve as fast as private goods"

From the "relief, recovery and reform" of Franklin D. Roosevelt's New Deal in the 1930's to the social reforms of Lyndon B. Johnson's Great Society in the 1960's, American government has always played an important role in facilitating the access of ordinary Americans to achieving the American Dream. But today, government services are clearly in need of a tune-up. Many doubt that the younger generations will be able to live as comfortably as their parents and grandparents did. And although Americans still look to their government for services such as public education, government reforms have not kept pace with the realities of our current volatile economy. **Since Sliced Bread** contestants want our government to be more responsive, innovative, productive, and to provide services that will give them greater value for their money:

- Anonymous in Ohio argues that modernizing mass transit and railroad freight infrastructure and converting public vehicle fleets to hybrid technology will reduce energy costs, create jobs, increase tax revenues, and replace lost manufacturing jobs (idea #20839).

- Donald B. in California suggests streamlining federal and state governments into one single HR department to manage all personnel matters (idea #13604).

- William M. of California suggested placing solar energy panels on the sides of schools to cut energy bills, and perhaps even selling the surplus energy to support the school (idea #13965), which combines the themes of making government more innovative, bringing new resources to our public schools, and creating a level-playing-field market for energy.

We have grown accustomed for many of our private goods—our computers, cars, and retail goods—to be of ever-higher quality and often at lower cost, due to the pressure of competition for our consumer dollars. In order for the public goods that we all share—such as education, roads, parks, and air quality—to improve just as rapidly, we need equal or greater commitment to innovation, efficiency, and quality in our public services.

Community Engagement:
"We're all in it together and doing our share"

Vibrant, strong communities are the fabric of the American Dream. When people are engaged in their communities, they feel more responsibility for the social and economic well-being of their neighbors. Pressured by the high cost of housing, health care, and caring for their children and parents, Americans feel that their resources are increasingly being stretched to the point where it is difficult for them to invest in their communities in a meaningful way. Nonetheless, the generous American spirit of cooperation and assistance is alive, and evident in the number of ideas that tackled family-friendly public policies that would help people offset the cost of child care, education, housing, and health care.

- **Since Sliced Bread** finalist Major Dan Clark of Florida proposes creating a civil work corps of youth who would serve 2-4 year terms on public works projects in exchange for college tuition (idea #20462).

- Anonymous in Maryland proposes allowing anyone to donate to a 529 for college savings, which allows philanthropies, local businesses, and communities to invest directly in funding a college education for deserving students (idea #21061).

- Jennifer G. in Tennessee wants to create non-profit community centers that would organize babysitting cooperatives that would offer lower-cost day care in exchange for volunteering for parents who would like to work part-time (idea #14143).

The values, trust, and mutual obligations lived within our communities—our neighborhoods, religious institutions, unions, and civic associations—are the foundations upon which an Opportunity Economy can be built, and Americans intuitively understand their vital importance.

American Dreaming:
Making a Difference

Re-tooling the American Dream poses some big questions, but "kitchen table" ideas like the 22,000 submitted to **Since Sliced Bread** can help to point the way to a better, more equitable future for Americans, and to a strong economy that keeps us heads-and-shoulders above our global competitors. We can still look to these "basics" of the American Dream as our compass in crafting 21st century policies for an Opportunity Economy:

- Americans should be able to achieve economic security and upward mobility through their hard work.

- Our children and grandchildren should have a better quality of life than we do.

- Anybody who wants to should be able to achieve a middle-class life, with a safe neighborhood, some savings to fall back on, and to own their own home.

- Everybody should have a fair shot at success, including access to high-quality, affordable education, regardless of the circumstances they were born into.

- Everybody deserves a second chance.

These guiding principles are at the core of many of the ideas submitted to **Since Sliced Bread,** and also of Hope Street Group's framework for achieving an Opportunity Economy in which the economy grows in tandem with the average American's access to economic opportunity. So, how do we keep these ideas alive and even put some into action? Participating in the **Since Sliced Bread** "folksonomy" is one step you can take. By helping rank and sort the ideas into categories, you can help make sure some of the best ideas are brought to light. You can also encourage your elected representatives to search for ideas by state (http://www2.sinceslicedbread.com/ideas/states), or send them your favorite **Since Sliced Bread** ideas directly. Another way is to get involved in Hope Street Group's unique open-source model of policy development and outreach (http://www.hopestreet-group.org/volunteer.htm). Hope Street Group is building a nation-wide constituency to develop and promote Opportunity Economics as a governing philosophy for the United States. Our members and volunteers are business executives, professionals, and entrepreneurs from across the country whose goal is to make equality of opportunity in a high-growth economy a reality for all Americans. We tap into the expertise and resources of the private sector in an unprecedented way to develop bold public policy innovations consistent with Opportunity Economics principles, and to create 'safe havens' for political leaders to embrace these bold policy innovations. Hope Street Group welcomes everyone who wants to develop, promote, and support ideas to achieve the American Dream for all.

Endnotes

1. "New Energy For America—The Apollo Jobs Report." Institute for America's Future, 2004. http://www.apolloalliance.org.

2. "New Energy For America—The Apollo Jobs Report." Institute for America's Future, 2004. http://www.apolloalliance.org.

3. "Putting Renewables to Work: How Many Jobs Can the Clean Energy Industry Generate?" Daniel Kammen, Renewable and Appropriate Energy Laboratory, UC Berkeley, 2004.

4. "Putting Renewables to Work: How Many Jobs Can the Clean Energy Industry Generate?" Daniel Kammen, Renewable and Appropriate Energy Laboratory, UC Berkeley, 2004.

5. "Putting Renewables to Work: How Many Jobs Can the Clean Energy Industry Generate?" Daniel Kammen, Renewable and Appropriate Energy Laboratory, UC Berkeley, 2004.

6. "Putting Renewables to Work: How Many Jobs Can the Clean Energy Industry Generate?" Daniel Kammen, Renewable and Appropriate Energy Laboratory, UC Berkeley, 2004.

7. "Putting Renewables to Work: How Many Jobs Can the Clean Energy Industry Generate?" Daniel Kammen, Renewable and Appropriate Energy Laboratory, UC Berkeley, 2004.

8. "Why Shouldn't Polluters Pay?" Jim Hightower, *The Hightower Lowdown*, April 2002.

9. "Snapshot: Indexing the minimum wage for inflation." Economic Policy Institute, December 2005.
http://www.epi.org/content.cfm/webfeatures_snapshots_20051221

10. http://www.businessweek.com/magazine/content/04_48/b3910096_mz021.htm

11. http://www.epinet.org/issuebriefs/224/ib224.pdf;
http://www.epinet.org/content.cfm/issueguides_minwage_minwagefaq

12. http://www.epinet.org/content.cfm/issueguides_minwage_minwagefaq

13. http://www.epinet.org/content.cfm/issueguides_minwage_minwagefaq

14. http://www.santafelivingwage.org/finalordinance.html

15. http://www.epi.org/issueguides/minwage/epi_minimum_wage_issue_guide.pdf;
http://www.epi.org/issueguides/minwage/epi_minimum_wage_issue_guide.pdf

16. Myth and Measurement: The New Economics of the Minimum Wage, David Card and Alan B. Kruger, Princeton University Press, 1997.

17. http://www.businessweek.com/magazine/content/04_48/b3910096_mz021.htm

18. "Leading The Way." *NEA Today*, National Education Association, May 2005.
http://www.nea.org/neatoday/0505/leading.html

19. "Insuring Inequality: The Privatization of Public Education in the U.S." Richard D. Vogel, *Monthly Review*, August 2005.
http://mrzine.monthlyreview.org/vogel190805.html

20. "Public Policy and the Enrollment Gap: The Impact on Higher Education." *Leads*, Center for Education Policy and Leadership (CEPAL), Spring 2004. http://www.education.umd.edu/EDPA/CEPAL/Leads/Spring%202004.pdf

21. "Achievement Gap Continues to Challenge Ideal of Equal Educational Opportunity." *AAC&U News*, The Association of American Colleges and Universities (AAC&U), March 2004. http://www.aacu-edu.org/aacu_news/AACUNews04/March04/facts_figures.cfm

22. "Achievement Gap Continues to Challenge Ideal of Equal Educational Opportunity." *AAC&U News*, The Association of American Colleges and Universities (AAC&U), March 2004. http://www.aacu-edu.org/aacu_news/AACUNews04/March04/facts_figures.cfm

23. "2004 Survey & Analysis of Teacher Salary Trends." American Federation of Teachers. http://www.aft.org/salary/

24. "The Condition of Education 2004." *Education Statistics Quarterly*, National Center for Education Statistics, 2004. http://nces.ed.gov/programs/quarterly/vol_6/1_2/7_1.asp

25. "Health Insurance Cost." National Coalition on Health Care, 2004. http://www.nchc.org/facts/cost.shtml

26. "Beyond Red vs. Blue." Survey Report, The Pew Research Center For The People And The Press, May 2005. http://people-press.org/reports/display.php3?ReportID=242

27. "Medicare: A National Treasure for Forty Years." Medicare Rights Center, July 2005. http://www.medicarerights.org/

28. "Medicare: A National Treasure for Forty Years." Medicare Rights Center, July 2005. http://www.medicarerights.org/

29. "Beyond Red vs. Blue." Survey Report, The Pew Research Center For The People And The Press, May 2005. http://people-press.org/reports/display.php3?ReportID=242 http://www.census.gov/prod/2006pubs/p60-231.pdf

30. "Paying More but Getting Less: Myths and the Global Case for U.S. Health Reform." Tom Daschle, Center for American Progress, November 2005. http://www.healthcare-now.org/orgresources.php?sid=4&subid=29

31. *International Journal of Health Services*, January 2004.

32. "The Facts." Americans for Health Care. http://www.americansforhealthcare.org/facts/groups/minorities.cfm http://www.census.gov/prod/2006pubs/p60-231.pdf

33. National Economic Council/Domestic Policy Council. The White House, February 29, 2000.

34. House Committee on Ways and Means; Census Bureau; Department of Labor.

35. "The Earned Income Tax Credit: Boosting Employment, Aiding the Working Poor." Robert Greenstein, Center on Budget and Policy Priorities, August 17, 2005. http://www.cbpp.org/7-19-05eic.htm

36. "The Earned Income Tax Credit: Boosting Employment, Aiding the Working Poor." Robert Greenstein, Center on Budget and Policy Priorities, August 17, 2005. http://www.cbpp.org/7-19-05eic.htm

37. "The Earned Income Tax Credit: Boosting Employment, Aiding the Working Poor." Robert Greenstein, Center on Budget and Policy Priorities, August 17, 2005. http://www.cbpp.org/7-19-05eic.htm

38. "The Earned Income Tax Credit: Boosting Employment, Aiding the Working Poor." Robert Greenstein, Center on Budget and Policy Priorities, August 17, 2005. http://www.cbpp.org/7-19-05eic.htm

39. "The Earned Income Tax Credit: Boosting Employment, Aiding the Working Poor." Robert Greenstein, Center on Budget and Policy Priorities, August 17, 2005. http://www.cbpp.org/7-19-05eic.htm

40. "The Earned Income Tax Credit: Boosting Employment, Aiding the Working Poor." Robert Greenstein, Center on Budget and Policy Priorities, August 17, 2005. http://www.cbpp.org/7-19-05eic.htm

41. "How Much Would A State Earned Income Tax Credit Cost?" Jason A. Levitis, Center on Budget and Policy Priorities, February 1, 2006. http://www.cbpp.org/2-1-06eic.htm

42. "The Earned Income Tax Credit: Boosting Employment, Aiding the Working Poor." Robert Greenstein, Center on Budget and Policy Priorities, August 17, 2005. http://www.cbpp.org/7-19-05eic.htm

43. Visual Teach. http://www.ttevisual.com

44. "RAND Study Links Higher Prices for Fruits and Vegetables to Excess Weight Gain Among School Children." RAND Corporation, October 5, 2005. http://www.rand.org/news/press.05/10.05.html

45. "NIH Releases Research Strategy to Fight Obesity Epidemic." *NIH News*, National Institutes of Health, August 24, 2004. http://www.nih.gov/news/pr/aug2004/niddk-24.htm

46. "Making Global Trade Work for People." Kamal Malhotra, UNDP/Earthscan, 2003.

47. "WTO Hands a Critical Victory to African Farmers." Gayle Smith and Susan Rice, *YaleGlobal*, Yale Center for the Study of Globalization, May 21, 2004. http://yaleglobal.yale.edu/display.article?id=3953

48. "Agricultural Subsidy." Wikipedia. http://en.wikipedia.org/wiki/Agricultural_subsidies/

49. "Small Farmers Seen Gaining Little from Subsidies." Barry James, *International Herald Tribune*, January 17, 2003.

50. "Fingers to the Bone: United States Failure to Protect Child Farmworkers." Human Rights Watch, 2000. http://www.hrw.org/reports/2000/frmwrkr/

51. "Biodiesel Facts." Fry-O-Diesel. http://www.fryodiesel.com/Bioodiesel%20facts.htm

52. "401(k) Action Initiative." Pension Rights Center. http://www.pensionrights.org/pages/401k_action.htm

53. "An Age of Shrinking Guarantees." *The Washington Post*, December 11, 2005. http://www.washingtonpost.com/wp-dyn/content/article/2005/12/10/AR2005121000252.html

54. "Tension Over Pensions." David R. Francis, *The Christian Science Monitor*, January 23, 2006. http://www.csmonitor.com/2006/0123/p17s02-cogn.html

55. "Retirement Security: Facts at a Glance." Economic Policy Institute, 2003 & 2005. http://www.epi.org/content.cfm/issueguides_retirement_facts/

56. "Retirement Security: Facts at a Glance." Economic Policy Institute, 2003 & 2005. http://www.epi.org/content.cfm/issueguides_retirement_facts/

57. "Retirement Security: Facts at a Glance." Economic Policy Institute, 2003 & 2005. http://www.epi.org/content.cfm/issueguides_retirement_facts/

58. "Retirement Security: Facts at a Glance." Economic Policy Institute, 2003 & 2005. http://www.epi.org/content.cfm/issueguides_retirement_facts/

59. "Retirement Security: Facts at a Glance." Economic Policy Institute, 2003 & 2005. http://www.epi.org/content.cfm/issueguides_retirement_facts/

60. "Infrastructure: The Global Dilemma." Dale Anne Reiss, Ernst & Young, January 9, 2006. http://www.ey.com/global/

61. The Apollo Alliance. http://www.apolloalliance.org/

62. "Schools In Need." Rebuild America's Schools. http://www.modernschools.org/

63. "Coalition Pushes Trades' Best Value Contracting." South Central Federation of Labor (WI), October 2005. http://scfl.freedmind.org/?ulnid=1107

64. http://www.prospect.org/webfeatures/1999/08/reich-r-08-11.html

65. "Lift the Cap on Social Security Taxes." John Miller, *Monthly Review*, July 2005. http://mrzine.monthlyreview.org/miller160705.html

66. "Lift the Cap on Social Security Taxes." John Miller, *Monthly Review*, July 2005. http://mrzine.monthlyreview.org/miller160705.html

67. "Lift the Cap on Social Security Taxes." John Miller, *Monthly Review*, July 2005. http://mrzine.monthlyreview.org/miller160705.html

68. "Lift the Cap on Social Security Taxes." John Miller, *Monthly Review*, July 2005. http://mrzine.monthlyreview.org/miller160705.html

69. "Higher Social Security Cap a Two-Edged Sword For GOP." Maeve Reston, *Pittsburgh Post-Gazette*, March 1, 2005. http://www.post-gazette.com/pg/05060/464453.stm

70. "Higher Social Security Cap a Two-Edged Sword For GOP." Maeve Reston, *Pittsburgh Post-Gazette*, March 1, 2005. http://www.post-gazette.com/pg/05060/464453.stm

71. http://www.census.gov/prod/2006pubs/p60-231.pdf
Care Without Coverage - Too Little, Too Late. Institute of Medicine, The National Academies Press, 2002. http://www.nchc.org/facts/coverage.shtml

72. "Rite of Passage? Why Young Adult Become Uninsured and How New Policies Can Help." Sara R. Collins, et. al., The Commonwealth Fund, 2005. http://www.cmwf.org/usr_doc/Collins_riteofpassage2006_649_ib.pdf

73. "Medical Records May Go Online." Mark S. Sullivan, *PC World*, August 23, 2004.

74. "News Release." Pediatric Academic Societies, May 15, 2005.

75. "U.S. Health Care Spending Reaches All-Time High: 15% of GDP." Pear, R., *The New York Times*, 9 January 2004, 3. http://www.nchc.org/facts/cost.shtml

76. Hidden Costs, Values Lost: Uninsurance in America. Institute of Medicine, The National Academies Press, June 17, 2003. http://www.nchc.org/facts/cost.shtml

77. http://www.pnhp.org/facts/singlepayer_myths_singlepayer_facts.php

78. "Sources of Coverage and Characteristics of the Uninsured: Analysis of the March 2004 Current Population Survey." Paul Fronstin, EBRI Issue Brief, Number 276, December 2004. (Last updated: March 21, 2005.) http://covertheuninsuredweek.org/databank/display.php?ChartID=7 http://www.census.gov/prod/2006pubs/p60-231.pdf

79. "A Brief History of the Civilian Conservation Corps." Civilian Conservation Corps. http://www.cccalumni.org/history1.html

80. http://www.dlc.org/ndol_ci.cfm?contentid=250409&kaid=115&subid=145

81. "Local Conservation Corps Help Young People Turn Their Lives Around." California Association of Local Conservation Corps (CALCC). http://www.californialocalconservationcorps.org/lcc.html

82. "Employment and Unemployment Among Youth Summary." U.S. Department of Labor, Bureau of Labor Statistics, August 19, 2005. http://www.bls.gov/news.release/youth.nr0.htm

83. http://www.ilo.org/public/english/bureau/inf/pr/2004/36.htm

84. "Digital Divisions." Pew Internet and American Life Project, October 5, 2005. http://www.pewinternet.org/pdfs/PIP_Digital_Divisions_Oct_5_2005.pdf http://www.pewinternet.org/pdfs/PIP_Digital_Divisions_Oct_5_2005.pdf

85. "Low Income Housing Goes Wireless." Associated Press, February 24, 2003. http://www.cnn.com/2003/TECH/internet/02/24/housing.hotspot.ap/

86. "Digital Divisions." Pew Internet and American Life Project, October 5, 2005. http://www.pewinternet.org/pdfs/PIP_Digital_Divisions_Oct_5_2005.pdf

87. "WiMax: An Efficient Tool to Bridge the Digital Divide." Guy Cayla, Stephane Cohen, and Didier Guigon, WiMAX Forum, November 2005. http://www.wimaxforum.org/news/downloads/WiMAX_to_Bridge_the_Digitaldivide.pdf

88. http://www.techsoup.org/learningcenter/networks/page5054.cfm

89. "New Orleans's New Connection." Jonathan Krim, *The Washington Post*, November 29, 2005. http://www.washingtonpost.com/wp-dyn/content/article/2005/11/28/AR2005112801773.html

90. http://www.pewinternet.org/pdfs/PIP_Digital_Divisions_Oct_5_2005.pdf

91. "America's Neighbors: The Affordable Housing Crisis and the People it Affects," National Low Income Housing Coalition, page 15. http://www.nlihc.org/research/neighbors.pdf

92. "How To Put Home Ownership Within the Reach of Most Working Americans." Duane Fleming, 2005.

93. "'Generation Debt'" Is Going Deep Into the Red." Vanessa Richardson, *MSNBC*, February 8, 2006. http://www.msnbc.msn.com/id/11238227/

94. "'Generation Debt'" Is Going Deep Into the Red." Vanessa Richardson, *MSNBC*, February 8, 2006. http://www.msnbc.msn.com/id/11238227/

95. "How To Put Home Ownership Within the Reach of Most Working Americans." Duane Fleming, 2005.

96. Independent Project Analysis. http://www.ipaglobal.com/index.asp

97. http://www.census.gov/Press-Release/www/2006/acspop_profile_highlights.html

98. "Congress Cuts Funding for Student Loans." Anne Marie Chaker, *The Wall Street Journal*, December 23, 2005.

99. "Publication 970." Internal Revenue Service.
http://www.irs.gov/publications/p970/ch06.html

100. "National Postsecondary Student Aid Study." U.S. Department of Education.

101. "Student Loan Cuts Put Kids in Financial Bind." Anita Burke, *Mail-Tribune* (Jackson, Oregon), February 16, 2006.

102. "A Letter to Parents: We Are Drowning in Debt." Elana Berkowitz and John Burton, Campus Progress, November 28, 2005.
http://www.campusprogress.org/features/663/a-letter-to-parents-we-are-drowning-in-debt

103. "Errors Across the Internet." *Consumer Reports*, March 2006.

104. "Errors Across the Internet." *Consumer Reports*, March 2006.

105. "Errors Across the Internet." *Consumer Reports*, March 2006.

106. "Higher Costs, Less Care." Ceci Connolly, *The Washington Post*, September 28, 2004.

107. "E-Prescribe Lowers Drug Costs, Errors." Katie Merx, *Detroit Free Press*, February 23, 2006.

108. http://www.infozine.com/news/stories/op/storiesView/sid/14153/

109. "Foundations of Finance." Federal Reserve Bank of New York.
http://www.ny.frb.org/education/money_management.html

110. "Students' Financial Ignorance a Major Parental Concern." Mary Deibel, *Scripps Howard News Service*, August 18, 2005.

111. http://ftp.ets.org/pub/corp/nclb.pdf

112. "Financial Literacy: Are We Improving?" Lewis Mandell, Jump$tart Coalition, 2004 edition.

113. http://projectonstudentdebt.org/files/pub/High_Hopes_Big_Debts.pdf

114. "Bankruptcy Bill Passed By House." Consumers Union, April 14, 2005.
http://www.consumersunion.org/

115. "Kids' Allowance Articles." Kids' Money.
http://www.kidsmoney.org/allart.htm#Drs

116. "Money Management 101: 13 Financial Tips for College Kids." Scott Reeves, *MSNBC*, August 31, 2004. http://www.msnbc.msn.com/id/5876473/

117. http://www.epi.org/content.cfm/webfeatures_snapshots_20060222

118. "2005 Skills Gap Report – A Survey of the American Manufacturing Workforce." National Association of Manufacturers, 2005.
http://www.nam.org/2005skillsgap/

119. "2005 Skills Gap Report – A Survey of the American Manufacturing Workforce." National Association of Manufacturers, 2005.
http://www.nam.org/2005skillsgap/

120. "Job Training's New Reality: You're On Your Own," Susan Aaron, "The Learning Coach," Monster Learning Educational Resources.
http://learning.monster.com/learning/resources?

121. "Earnings Premium For Skilled Workers Down Sharply In Recent Years." Lawrence Mishel and Jared Bernstein, Economic Policy Institute, February 2006. http://www.epinet.org/content.cfm?id=2282

122. "Reinventing Unions." *Blueprint Magazine*, Democratic Leadership Council, June 2000.

123. "Las Vegas As A Workers' Paradise." Harold Meyerson, *American Prospect*, January 2004. http://www.prospect.org/print/V15/1/meyerson-h.html

124. "Ridding Neighborhoods of Abandoned Housing." Miriam Hipchen, *The New Democrat*, Democratic Leadership Council, December 20, 2000. http://www.dlc.org/ndol_ci.cfm?kaid=114&subid=236&contentid=2831

125. "The High Cost of Credit: Disparities in High-priced Loans to Minority Homeowners in 125 American Cities." ACORN, Sept. 27, 2005. http://www.acorn.org/index.php?id=9758

126. "Reusing Forgotten Urban Land: The Genesee County Urban Land Redevelopment Initiative." Daniel T. Kildee, *Housing Facts & Findings*, Fannie Mae Foundation, 2004. http://www.fanniemaefoundation.org/programs/hff/pdf/HFF_v6i2.pdf

127. "Shrinking Detroit Has 12,000 Abandoned Homes." Agence France-Presse, 2004. http://www.theallineed.com/news/0508/146570.htm

128. "Freddie Mac's 'Summer of Homeownership' to Target Foreclosed HUD Properties in Baltimore." Freddie Mac, July 9, 2001. http://www.freddiemac.com/news/archives2001/rescuedhomes.htm

129. "Rehabilitation Mortgage Insurance (Section 203(k))." U.S. Department of Housing and Urban Development. http://www.hud.gov/offices/hsg/sfh/203k/203k--df.cfm

130. "Why Small Businesses Fail: U.S. Small Business Administration." Robert Longley. http://usgovinfo.about.com/od/smallbusiness/a/whybusfail.htm

131. "Small Business." Wikipedia. http://en.wikipedia.org/wiki/Small_business

132. "Small Business." Wikipedia. http://en.wikipedia.org/wiki/Small_business

133. "What Fannie Mae Does." Fannie Mae FAQ, April 13, 2006. http://www.fanniemae.com/faq/231001a.jhtml

134. "Small Consolation: The Dubious Benefits of Small Business for Job Growth and Wages." Dale Belman, Erica L. Groshen, David W. Stevens, and Julia Lane, Economic Policy Institute, 1998. http://www.epinet.org/studies/small_consolation-1998-FULL.pdf

135. "Get the Basics on Army, Navy, and Air Force ROTC." College Board. http://www.collegeboard.com/article/0,3868,4-24-0-36978,00.html

136. "AmericCorps Civilian Program Faces $22 Million Budget Cut." Christopher Lee, *The Washington Post*, February 28, 2006.

137. "Alumni Outline Barriers To Service." Joy Karugu, *The Daily Princetonian*, February 27, 2006.

138. "Federal Brain Drain." Partnership for Public Service, November 21, 2005. http://www.ourpublicservice.org/research/research_show.htm?doc_id=320870

139. "Federal Brain Drain." Partnership for Public Service, November 21, 2005. http://www.ourpublicservice.org/research/research_show.htm?doc_id=320870

140. "Creating a New Army of Patriots." John Kerry for President. http://web.archive.org/web/20040210043828/www.johnkerry.com/issues/natservice/

141. "Educating for Active Citizenship: Service-Learning, School-Based Service, and Civic Engagement." Corporation for National & Community Service, 2005. http://www.nationalservice.gov/pdf/06_0323_SL_briefing_factsheet.pdf

142. http://www.epi.org/content.cfm/bp175

143. "The Wage Squeeze and Higher Health Care Costs." Sylvia Allegretto and Jared Bernstein, Economic Policy Institute, January 27, 2006.

144. "Health Costs Will Cause More Strikes." David Lazarus, *San Francisco Chronicle*, December 23, 2005.

145. "GM, Auto Workers Reach Deal on Health Costs." *Associated Press*, October 17, 2005.

146. "U.S. Companies To Pay 10 Percent More For Health Benefits in 2006." Think Progress, Oct. 10, 2005.
http://thinkprogress.org/2005/10/10/health-costs-2006/

147. ""Toyota To Build 100,000 Vehicles Per Year in Woodstock, Ont." Steve Erwin, *Canadian Press*, February 14, 2006.

148. "Facts on Health Insurance Coverage." National Coalition on Health Care, 2004. http://www.nchc.org/facts/coverage.shtml

149. "Facts on Health Insurance Coverage." National Coalition on Health Care, 2004. http://www.nchc.org/facts/coverage.shtml

150. "Facts on Health Insurance Coverage." National Coalition on Health Care, 2004. http://www.nchc.org/facts/coverage.shtml

Index

Gen 2/15 TD